WHATEVER IT TAKES

WHATEVER IT TAKES
10 CHALLENGES TO INSPIRE YOUR FAITH

Delme Linscott

Whatever it Takes
Self - Published in November 2015
www.LivingInGrace.co.za
Text: © Delme Linscott
Editing done by team of friends
Layout and Publishing by Lara Moran of Lara Moran Designs.

Cover design: Paul de Villiers
Printed and bound by Kendall & Strachan Printhouse, Victoria Road, Pietermaritzburg, South Africa.

ISBN: 978-0-620-67474-4

Dedication

For Barry Schooling – your smile lives on in our hearts. May you surf the waves of God's endless grace.

For the many people in our community struggling with Cancer. You are doing *whatever it takes* to get through your treatment sessions and to fight for another day. We salute you! May God grant you His strength and Grace today.

CONTENTS

Five Words of Thanks 9

Foreword – Xavier Moran 11

First thoughts – Laying the foundation. 13

1. Frantic for change – Something is not right within me. 19

2. For the sake of a cause – We can make a difference. 31

3. Fame – Is it really worth it? 43

4. Fortune – The mirage at the end of the rainbow. 55

5. Forgiveness – Is it possible to forgive others? 71

6. Family – Living with those who know your dark side. 85

7. Friendship – Two are better than one. 99

8. Faith – Persevering until the end. 115

9. Fellowship – Surviving prickly issues in the church. 133

10. Final Word – Making things crystal clear. 149

11. Finding Courage – Stories to inspire us to do whatever it takes. 157

References 179

Five Words of Thanks

There Are Angels in Our Midst

John Maxwell once remarked that "you can't do anything that counts unless you have countability. Teammates must be able to count on each other when it really counts."

In my efforts to complete this book, I have had a team of people that I could count on. They have surrounded me with their prayers, encouragement and support. I am overwhelmed by their love and inspiration. These are my five words of Thanks:

1. My awesome wife, Kim, has sacrificially allowed me time away from our family duties to read, write and edit this book. Along with our 3 boys, Declan, Nathan and Joshua, she has borne the brunt of my absence and for that gift I am grateful. My hope is that they have seen some of the *whatever it takes* fruit in my own life.

2. My extended family have always believed in me and their unequivocal support is a blessing in my life. I thank you all for your love and encouragement. To Hylton, Di, Sharlé, Tim, Erin, David, Phyllis, Nadine and Blair, I say Ngiyabonga!

3. When I wrote my first book, *Living Oceans Apart,* there were a team of amazing friends who surrounded me during that experience. Many of those same people, plus numerous others, have had an invaluable input into this book – take a bow, Gareth Killeen, Xavier and Lara Moran, Andy Thomas, Paul and Izzi DeVilliers, Quin and Ty Bache, Mark Duncan, Mike Howell, Tim Stephen, Russell Norman and Jenny Stainer.

A special thanks needs to go out to Xavier Moran for your hours of editing and your gracious Foreword. I also want to make special mention of Lara Moran, for helping with the publishing and type-setting and Paul DeVilliers for designing the cover. Your creativity is inspiring and I thank God for your gifts and talents.

There have been a number of generous friends, who have helped me pay for the publication of this book. They have asked to remain anonymous and I respect their wishes, but do want to acknowledge their generosity. God bless you.

4. I also owe a great debt to my friends at Wesley Methodist Church, who have journeyed with me over the years and have allowed me the space to explore my writing. I also thank my colleagues, Collin, Russell, Kim and Michél for your understanding, creative input and prayers. It is a pleasure serving alongside you.

5. I thank the Lord for His unlimited Grace in my life. I owe everything I have to you, Jesus. Soli Deo Gloria.

FOREWORD

Through honest reflection any follower of Jesus would own up to the gross disparity that exists between their professed belief and what is observed in their everyday interactions with people, how they spend their money, use their time and their private thoughts. There is a gap and we are all aware of it. It is evident to non-believers, who at times site the gap to justify their unbelief and to believers who often remain silently weighed down by the difference. It is into this gap, this disparity, that the work of 'Whatever it Takes' speaks with challenging clarity.

As a local church pastor and family man (and Manchester United supporter), Delme is at the coalface of dealing with this gap. In his desire to be a faithful leader in the church and loving husband and father at home, he is preoccupied with translating truth into everyday practice, not only for himself but also for fellow believers who find themselves lost in the darkness of the disparity; desperate for any form of illumination which would help them enter the promised new freedom of life in Christ Jesus.

To the sincere seeker and devoted pilgrim, Delme ushers a renewed challenge to choose life in Christ with an unreserved determination and passion. With pastoral care, Delme invites us all to re-examine where our faith lives, and in so doing, giving opportunity for the Holy Spirit to convict, heal, restore and lead us into the promised life in Christ. With compassionate honesty, Delme considers the risk of a pale expression of the Light of the World to a world in need, sounding a sobering warning to a church, a family and any individual who remains slave to their former old life whilst having accept new life in Jesus.

The additional questions at the end of each chapter further indicate Delme's desire for these words on a page to gain new expression in the life of the reader. As a fellow sojourner, I believe the message of this book to be timeous at a time when social instability, economic hardship, and much uncertainty are a daily header, reminding the people called 'Christian' of their divine commission to be living expressions of hope, peace and love.

Xavier Moran

Introduction

FIRST THOUGHTS

LAYING THE FOUNDATION

"I do not believe in a fate that falls on men however they act; but I do believe in a fate that falls on them unless they act."

- G. K CHESTERTON

Writing a book usually starts with a simple idea. I have found that once that initial idea pops into my mind, it begins to grow and develop from all angles. If it is fed with inspiration and disciplined attention it will slowly take root in the soil of creativity. This is how I believe this book came about. One day I was driving down the street, thinking about nothing in particular, when a song began playing on the radio. As I listened to the song by Lifehouse, I heard the phrase 'whatever it takes' sung a few times and soon I was arrested by these three words:

Whatever

It

Takes.

I could not stop these words from crashing into my world. As hard as I tried to think about something else, the phrase *whatever it takes* kept running through my mind. It was as if the Spirit of God had been waiting to get my attention and the words in the song had been the catalyst for this. Idea after idea sparked off into a fire of imagination, whilst the song continued to play quietly in the background,

"I'll do whatever it takes
To turn this around
I know what's at stake

I know I've let you down
And if you give me a chance
and believe that I can change
I'll keep us together whatever it takes." - Lifehouse

And so, through somewhat of a strange experience, the journey of this book began. Countless confirmations later I felt convicted to make time available to knuckle down and explore writing this book. In a sense, I have taken the measured approach and have preached on a few of these themes during the past 5 years. This has allowed me to go deeper into the idea and truly test the validity of connecting *whatever it takes* to our personal faith journey. And so in the end, this provocative phrase kept coming back to me in the form of a question:

"Are you willing to do whatever it takes?"

It intrigues me that we are willing to go to incredible lengths to maintain certain lifestyles or to attain wealth or fame, but when it comes to the crucial things in life, we are not willing to go to similar lengths. Perhaps we don't know how to do this, but deep down, I fear that many of us just don't want to!

A few months ago we experienced a power outage in our suburb. Once the electricians had discovered that one of the transformers had blown up they searched for the cause of the fault and eventually they stumbled across the charred remains of a Hadeda Ibis – commonly known in South Africa as a Hadeda. The poor bird had obviously chosen the wrong cable to rest on and in an instant the bird had become a 'burnt offering.' This large noisy bird had inadvertently been the cause of much panic and consternation. In one second, the Hadeda had effectively impacted the lives of thousands of people. One bird – thousands of headaches!

This is what transpires when individuals do all they can to please themselves and when they make selfish decisions. It amazes me that people can make a decision to do *whatever it takes* to get what they want, but they seldom think of the consequences of their actions. In the ensuing chapters I will share a number of illustrations pertaining to what I am suggesting.

When we believe that we "deserve something" or "need something" and we don't count the cost, you can be sure that many lives will be drastically impacted. I will do *whatever it takes* to get what I feel I need, but when things go horribly wrong I am unwilling to do *whatever it takes* to make things right.

History is littered with courageous men and women who have faced insurmountable challenges and yet have been determined to do whatever it takes to defend their honour, seek justice, fight for their families or even just to advance a cause they felt was worth dying for. There is something heroic about these people, something that stirs within the souls of every one of us and this breathes inspiration into our very being. Life is more than just surviving – it is about dreaming that victory is at hand, that light can defeat darkness, that love wins out over evil and that we can live another day.

For Christ-followers, this idea proves an even greater challenge for us. The reason I say this is because Jesus Christ, the very person we seek to model our lives on, lived a *whatever it takes* life. In fact, it underpinned everything He did! This is most clearly evident when He allowed Roman soldiers to nail Him to a wooden cross. We should never see the Cross of Calvary as a symbol of defeat, but rather the greatest display of *whatever it takes* ever seen. The Son of God was willing to die on the cross, in order to restore humanity into a relationship with our God. This was more than just mere words – it was the ultimate example of laying down a life for others.

In his work, *Jesus' plan for a new world*, Richard Rohr reminds us that in the book of Acts there is a phrase used to describe the new movement, which was upsetting the world order. [1] The Christians were labelled as "the people who have been turning the whole world upside down..." (Acts 17: 6-7). Living out our lives as Christians is about turning the world upside down; it is about doing *whatever it takes* to live for Jesus.

Taking the decision to do *whatever it takes* is not a brief flutter in our heart, but a deep-rooted, gut-wrenching, mind-blowing commitment to persevere, even against all odds. We will carry on until the goal is achieved, evil is vanquished and the mountain has been summited.

Nothing will stop us.

"Taking the decision to do whatever it takes is not a brief flutter in our heart, but a deep-rooted, gut-wrenching, mind-blowing commitment to persevere, even against all odds."

No one will get in our way.

No obstacle will be too great.

We will do *whatever it takes*.

So, I invite you into these three dangerous words - *Whatever it takes*. As you read this book, may you wrestle with their meaning for your life and I pray that they may present a deep challenge to your faith. I hope that you will be changed after reading these pages and that you will be inspired to re-ignite your faith journey.

Lastly, can I suggest that you take your time in reading each chapter and deliberately chew on the questions I have offered for reflection? Personally I feel that this book will prove most rewarding when read slowly and without distraction. Thanks again for taking the time to read these words. May you be blessed.

Living in Grace

Delme

one

FRANTIC FOR CHANGE

SOMETHING IS NOT RIGHT WITHIN ME

"Everybody thinks of changing humanity and nobody thinks of changing himself."

\- LEO TOLSTOY

"There comes a moment that defines winning from losing. The true warrior understands and seizes the moment by giving effort so intensive and so intuitive that it could be called one from the heart."

\- PAT RILEY

Over the years I have had the privilege of meeting people from all walks of life. The ministry has given me the gift of hearing the stories of many different people. One of the things that continuously amazes me is that people are willing to do *whatever it takes* to obtain certain material things in life, but they are not so energised to pursue the truly important things.

Don Marquis argues that "ours is a world where people don't know what they want and are willing to go through hell to get it."[2] This is true on so many levels. The goals we often strive for don't end up satisfying us when we reach them. And so, the question of 'what are the truly important things in life' is open to debate. I suggest that there are a few key areas we should consider including on this list, such as: Family, Friendships, Faith, and Forgiveness, amongst others. I strongly believe that if we paid closer attention to these focal points, our communities would be in better shape. Our society seems to be disintegrating all around us and so we don't have the luxury of doing nothing to address these important areas.

Many years ago a colleague in Cape Town shared a story with me that has often come back to my mind. He had a man come to see him about his marriage. He was a successful sportsman and clearly he was a disciplined individual – able to do *whatever it takes* to be successful in his chosen field. No one would be able to question his dedication and passion in this area of his life. However, when it came to his marriage, things weren't going well, but he just wasn't willing to fight for it. There were no clear reasons for this couple to get divorced, but he just felt trapped and so this became the only way out for him. The struggle with his decision was this - here you have a person who has the ability to do *whatever it takes* in one arena of his life (this was a proven fact), but in another situation, he chooses not to do *whatever it takes* in his marriage .

But this man's story is not unique in our society. There are thousands like him, desperate for change, but they get caught up in making painful choices. Perhaps we are even able to identify with his story on some level. We would do well to ask ourselves these crucial questions:

-      How far are we willing to go for something?

-      Will we do *whatever it takes* for our family, or for a friend, or even for God?

Sometimes life deals us a difficult hand and we have no sign of hope at all. Our desperation can make us do anything, hoping for a change. This was the case in the story of Mohamed Bouazizi. I read about his story in an article entitled, "The slap that went all the way around the world."[3] During a freedom protest in Tunisia, young Mohamed was slapped in the face by a female police officer, who was simply trying to calm him down. Although she was trying to bring order in the chaos, her action became the proverbial tipping point for Mohamed. It pushed him over the edge.

As an act of complete sacrifice, this young freedom fighter set himself alight as a protest against the government and its policies. Yes, you did read correctly – he doused himself in fuel, set himself on fire and became a human torch in the streets of Tunisia. His act of self-sacrifice proved to be a crucial moment in the ending of Tunisian dictatorship. Because of Mohamed's extreme action, this story has become known as the 'slap that went all the way around the world!'

Here is my point in this: *Whatever it takes* can never be in a half measure. If we are desperate for change in our lives and circumstances, we must expect to pay some price. It probably won't be as drastic as our young freedom fighter from Tunisia, but all good things come at a cost.

If we read the Scriptures we will see that they contain numerous stories of people who embraced the *whatever it takes* attitude. There are two particular incidents that are worth noting at this point. One of these is from the prophet Nehemiah and the other from the Gospel of Luke.

Nehemiah had risen through the ranks in Persia, earning a comfortable position in the land, when he heard that things back in Jerusalem were not good. "Those in the province…are in great trouble and disgrace. The wall of Jerusalem is broken down, and its gates have been burned with fire" (Nehemiah 1:3).

Before we look at Nehemiah's actual response, it is worth noting what he didn't do. He never fell to the ground, whingeing and moaning, shouting out the following comments:

- "Well, someone better do something about it!"
- "What is wrong with those people in Jerusalem?"
- "I can't believe our government officials!"
- "If I were there, I would ……blah, blah!"

If we are honest, our society is full of complainers, gripers, moaners, and armchair- referees. It is easy to sit back and whinge about stuff, because we are all desperate for change, but our society doesn't need more moaners – do we? What we need are more people willing to do something to bring about change. We need more people like Nehemiah, willing to do *whatever it takes* to effect a change.

Nehemiah's reaction to the destruction of the walls in Jerusalem is profound. His decision changed the course of history. As a man of action he took up the challenge of restoring the city of Jerusalem. His response is seen in 3 clear steps:

1. He began with an intimate prayer before God (Nehemiah 1:5-11)
2. Then he approached the King of Persia, boldly asking him for the chance to go home (Nehemiah 2:1-10).
3. Lastly, he bought a bus ticket and set about travelling back to Jerusalem (… well, there were no buses running that day, so he took a Camel instead).

Here is a part of Nehemiah's inspiring speech:

"Then I said to them, "You see the trouble we are in: Jerusalem lies in ruins, and its gates have been burned with fire. Come let us rebuild the wall of Jerusalem, and we will no longer be in disgrace." I also told them about the gracious hand of my God upon me and what the king had said to me." (Nehemiah 2:17-18)

Even when Nehemiah and his team met resistance from the nay-sayers, Sanballat, Tobiah and Geshem, they weren't put off by their criticism. Through Nehemiah's leadership the people of Israel recognised the need for change and they were willing to do whatever they could to bring this about.

What Israel lacked at this time was not more complainers and whingers, lamenting their bad situation, but rather they desperately needed leadership. The leadership of the Israelites had been found wanting and it seemed as if there was no one willing to lead the nation with courage and conviction. Perhaps this sounds very familiar for many of us living around the world – certainly South Africa finds herself in a situation of leadership crisis at the moment.

Nehemiah's story doesn't end with one surge to the finish line - it was much more complicated than that. The team of builders met an ever increasing attitude of resistance. The resistance was coupled with dangerous threats and curses. Yet, it was Nehemiah's words of encouragement, his commitment to prayer and his visible leadership strengths that allowed the wall to be rebuilt in just 52 days.

> *"To stand in the gap means to place no limits on how fully God may use you"*

And so the testimony of Nehemiah is that God helps him to effect change in a desperate situation. It is not entirely Nehemiah's work as he needed the help of many others, but certainly his leadership inspires the community to do *whatever it takes* to restore the city.

In his book *Stand in the Gap*, David Bryant challenges us to live a *whatever it takes* lifestyle in the presence of God.[4] He says, 'to stand in the Gap means to place no limits on how fully God may use you, or for whose sake. It means that, as God directs you, you are willing to take on any role, any time, any place, by any means, with anyone and at any cost that will help close the Gap..."

The prophet Ezekiel said a similar thing, thousands of years before David Bryant:
"I looked for a person among them who would build up the wall and stand before me in the gap on behalf of the land" (Ezekiel 22:30).

There will come moments in our lives where we recognise the need for change or to stand up for something. There may be others who could do this, but perhaps God brings it to our attention, because he wants us to make a call to step forward. Isaiah's encounter with God in worship is such a moment. Isaiah may have looked around for someone else to step forward, but in the end he says "Here I am Lord, send me!"

In 2012, my friends Peter Grassow and Mark Duncan recognised that Pietermaritzburg had a major problem with our street children. Like many cities in the world, there wasn't a proper facility for these children and so instead of being the complainers, Peter and Mark decided to do something about it. In that year, they committed to run 5 km's a day, for 300 days in the year. That is 6 out of 7 days - every week of the year. They did all of this to raise funds and awareness for the I-Care project and for children living on the streets. Pietermaritzburg can get fairly cold in winter, but these two guys were willing to do *whatever it takes* to bring about change in the lives of others. They are ordinary guys willing to make a big difference for God.

Early on in the chapter I promised you two stories from the Bible. The second one is from Luke's gospel and it known as the 'woman who touched Jesus' cloak' (Luke 8:40 – 48). This is an account of a person who was desperate for change in her life and was willing to do *whatever it takes* to make it happen.

This un-named woman had been suffering from an ailment for 12 years. Her ailment made her unclean in her religious community and an outcast in society. Just imagine living like that for a moment? No contact with other people for 12 years and not because of her choice - her isolation was imposed upon her.

However, we need to commend this woman for being a determined believer – she was a fighter – and she was not going to let one more opportunity slip by. Remembering that she had spent all she had on doctors her hope is turned to Jesus. As Jesus comes to town she thinks to herself, "He is my only hope!"

Risking everything she joins the crowds with a clear purpose – to get to Jesus. Disguising herself she draws nearer and nearer to him. As Jesus is busy with the crowds, she silently pushes her way through the crowds and then doing all she can she reaches for his robe.

Perhaps we can imagine what is going on in her mind as she reaches out to Jesus – anyone of the following thoughts may have crossed her mind:

"I wonder if he will notice me?"

"I wonder if this will work?"

"This is my last chance!"
She does what it takes to get into touching distance of Jesus and when she feels the texture of his clothes, she is healed instantly – Jesus changes her life forever!

Most of us who are reading this book are blessed with choices. We get to choose on a number of levels – relationships, places of worship, shops to go to, places of study, cars to drive, places to live, gadgets to buy, careers to pursue, sports teams to support and so on. We have plenty of options. It is my prayer that we would allow God's spirit to guide us to make the right choices and to genuinely do *whatever it takes* in the 'right places' in our lives.

For me, the concept of "choosing well", means choosing the things that have eternal value. However, this often means going against convention and taking the 'road less travelled.' The following story by Floyd McClung illustrates this point:

> "There was a woman whose son had been killed in World War II. She herself was a devout Christian, but her son had long since turned his back on the church. When the army shipped his body home, she went to the priest and asked that her son be buried in the church cemetery.
>
> This put the priest in a dilemma. He knew how much it meant to the woman to have her son buried in the cemetery, but the law of the church said that only members in good standing could be buried there. Finally, with great sorrow, he had to tell her, "I'm sorry. I can't do it. As much as I would like to, I just can't."
>
> The mother went away broken-hearted and the priest agonised over the disappointment he had caused this good woman. He tossed and turned all night, thinking about it. Early the next morning he called her. "I want you to have your son's body brought over here," he said. "I want you to have him buried just outside the wall of the cemetery."
>
> "But I don't want him buried outside the cemetery," she said. "I want him buried inside!"

The priest simply said, "Trust me."

So the woman had her son buried just outside the wall of the cemetery, as the priest had instructed her. The next day she came back to tend the grave and found to her amazement that the wall had been rebuilt to go around the burial site. The law of the church said he could not be buried inside the cemetery. But no law prohibited the cemetery wall from being moved. Because of his love, the priest had found a way." [5]

Our communities may be desperate for change and perhaps we are being called upon to be part of that change. Is it not time to start doing what we can to move beyond our comfort zones?

TIME OF REFLECTION

Before we look at a new theme in the next chapter, here is a challenge for us to consider:

1. Has God been speaking to you about something that needs to change in your own life? If yes, then are you willing to do *whatever it takes* to make this happen?

2. Have you sensed a growing restlessness in your spirit of late? What could God be leading you towards? Does this excite you or fill you with fear?

3. How do you respond to Augustine's comment?
    "You have made us for yourself, O Lord, and our heart is restless until it rests in you."

4. Perhaps God has been stirring up something in your heart for a while and you have been putting it off. Maybe a calling to serve in

an area or perhaps an idea that seems bigger than you think you can handle. Ask yourself,

- "If this is of God, then surely God will give me all I need to accomplish this task?" Are you willing to step up to the plate and say "Lord, I am your man or woman?" I am willing to do this for you."

two

FOR THE SAKE OF A CAUSE

WE CAN MAKE A DIFFERENCE

"In this world of so much pain, why have I been blessed with so much?"

- GARY HAUGEN

"We will abandon it all, for the sake of the cause."

- STEVE CURTIS CHAPMAN

Sometimes we need a particular cause or project to motivate us to move beyond ourselves and to consider doing *whatever it takes* for the benefit of others. William Wilberforce found this to be true in his lifelong struggle to end slavery in Britain. It was truly a cause beyond his own resources, yet Wilberforce was deeply challenged by the evil of slavery and this energised him to become a champion for the rights of slaves.

Wilberforce's Christian principles gave him resolve in fighting to abolish slavery. He believed that freedom for every human being was not a privilege for a few human beings, but rather a God given right for every person. And he was willing to do all he could to make this dream possible. In one of his famous speeches, Wilberforce challenged his community by saying:

"You may choose to look the other way but you can never say again that you did not know."[6]

The story of *The Shetland Bus* is another incredible reminder of how a group of people can do extraordinary things for the sake of a great cause.

During the Second World War, a group of young men went to sea in fishing trawlers with one major mission – to save the lives of people in Norway. They shuttled people, in and out of Norway, supplying them with weapons, radios and other equipment, and then 'bussed' ordinary civilians out of the Nazi occupied country. They carried out these operations from 1941 until the German occupation ended on 8 May 1945.

These treacherous crossings were usually made during the winter months, as they could operate under a protective cover of darkness. The crew and their passengers had to endure extremely hazardous conditions in the North Sea, often with no lights, and with the constant risk of being discovered by the German forces. The fear of being captured was something these men had to live with on a daily basis, but they managed to disguise themselves so effectively that they avoided any detection.

These extraordinary young men never viewed themselves as heroes, but when you considered what they did, at great risk to their own lives, it is remarkable. One of these young men, Leif Andreas Larsen is regarded as the most well-known of the Shetland Bus crew. Over a period of four years he made 52 trips to Norway, and in doing so became one of the most highly-decorated Allied naval officers of the War. Leif Larsen is a prime example of someone willing to do *whatever it takes* to save others and to defend his country.

Just a few decades later, Martin Luther King Jnr made a strong statement on the extremity of our love in action. He wrote: "Was not Jesus an extremist for love? So the question is not whether we will be extremists, but what kind of extremists we will be?"

This is a radical question, well worth ruminating on for a while – what kind of extremists will we be?

In a powerful sense, the question that Martin Luther King Jnr poses is the same question that Geoffrey Canada found himself asking. What kind of extreme love would it take to change the lives of poor children—not one by one, but rather in big numbers, and in a way that could be replicated nationwide? This burning question led him to create the *Harlem Children's Zone,* a ninety-seven-block laboratory in central Harlem where he is testing new and sometimes controversial ideas about poverty in America.

He ended up with the following conclusion: "if you want poor kids to be able to compete with their middle-class peers, you need to change everything in their lives—their schools, their neighbourhoods, even the child-rearing practices of their parents." Appropriately, his experiment has been reported in an article entitled: *Whatever It Takes.* Geoffrey Canada is an inspiring example of one person doing *whatever it takes* to change the lives of others. Included in the article on the *Harlem Children's Zone,* is a reflection on this remarkable experiment:

> "This is an inspired portrait not only of Geoffrey Canada but of the parents and children in Harlem who are struggling to better their lives, often against great odds. Carefully researched and deeply affecting, this is a dispatch from inside the most daring and potentially transformative social experiment of our time."[7]

Often we want to know what motivates individuals like Wilberforce, Larsen, King or Geoffrey Canada. What ignites the fire in their belly? Is there some key ingredient that we could search for and adopt in our own lives? I am certain it was because they were absolutely convinced of what they believed in and they were willing to do *whatever it takes* to effect change. We have to believe that we can make a difference, before we begin to try.

The true story of Joseph Lister is another reminder of how one person can change the lives of many. He was the first person to experiment with antiseptic materials to clean surgical equipment in the 1860's. He was distressed by the high number of people who were dying after surgery and so he sought a solution to this dilemma. He was ridiculed and taunted by his peers, but he refused to be dissuaded and he never backed down. In the end, it was his willingness to do *whatever it takes* to save lives that brought antiseptic medicines to our world. Many antiseptic materials are simply taken for granted today, but if it weren't for his perseverance and courage we may still be subject to unclean surgical instruments in our hospitals and a lower chance of survival.

"If we have Jesus Christ, we have enough!"

Before we get side-tracked into the glamour of going the extra mile for an important cause, I want to bring us back to my original premise. In my opening chapter I argued that many people are willing to do *whatever it takes* in other areas of their lives, but not often in the arena of faith. Sometimes people are even confronted with their own mortality in pursuing a worthy cause, yet they still ignore the voice of God, calling for them to honour their families or even their relationship with Him.

I am not saying that we shouldn't fight for specific causes confronting our community, but we should always seek to honour our Godly mandate first. If I have responded to the call of God, then it is likely that God will raise me up to be the champion for someone else. But, I strongly believe in getting first things first – that should be our main priority.

Gary Burge makes the following honest remarks: "Are there areas of modern life that need to be violated in the name of God so that God's person and justice can be seen by everyone? When I think of past examples of this, such as the Abolitionist Movement to end slavery, I am comfortable and show open support for their heroism. But rarely do I have the courage to recreate the spiritual heroism demanded today."

This is so true of many of us, we know that something is not right in our communities or families or churches, yet we are reluctant to do *whatever it takes* to make a change. We can blame fear, or inadequacy, or lack of education, but in truth, if we have Jesus Christ, we have enough. Jesus is calling us to abandon all and follow him. He has not called us to be pre-qualified before we follow him.

Our Church community supports a few social projects around the city of Pietermaritzburg. One of these is called *Eden Kids*. Pastor Joel Ruttenberg saw a need for godly care to be provided for the children of the Jika-Joe informal settlement and so has set up this project. He helps children plant their own vegetable gardens, provides mentorship to some of the older kids, offers Christian teaching to the community and gives hope to many people. And the beauty of this project lies in its location – it is less than 7 kilometres from our Church, on the fringes of the city. One doesn't have to travel to the ends of the earth for the sake of a cause!

The remarkable story of Howard Bell illustrates how a person may be able to achieve two goals – doing what it takes for God's glory, as well as serving another cause. To be honest, I had never heard of Howard Bell until one day I came across his book *More than a conquerors* in a local Church library. His story is truly inspiring. At the age of one, Howard was diagnosed with spinal muscular atrophy and his doctors told his parents that he would be fortunate to live to be five. However, together with God's help and the care of his family, Howard beat the odds and went on to achieve many things, despite his disability.

Although he only weighed a mere 20 kilograms, Howard put his life in God's hands and has been willing to do *whatever it takes* to serve God. He went on to graduate as valedictorian from South Mountain Community College and is the founder of "You Can Foundation of American," which raises funds to buy handicapped-equipped vehicles for people with disabilities.

This is what Howard had to say about what he has achieved:

> "My ministry is not based on what I can do, although God has enabled me to do many wonderful things. My ministry is based on what God can do – through me, and through anyone he touches. Of all the wonderful things God is allowing me to do, the most wonderful is to be able to serve His people and let them know that in spite of any circumstances, and no matter what their problems may be – emotional or physical – we are more than conquerors through Christ. There is no problem too big for God."[8]

This is further proof for me, that when we combine a worthy cause with a committed person and a big God, we can see miraculous results. If you like, the following simple formula could describe the combination of all these factors.

Committed person + worthy cause + Big God = Miracles

I know that I have completely simplified this concept, but it may help us to grasp what I am getting at. Our God has placed us in locations where there are worthy causes. God is looking for a committed person to stand up and to be used for change. Is that person going to be you?

Early in 2010 I had the privilege of attending a motivational talk by Lewis Pugh. I had already done some research into his achievements and had greatly admired his willingness to go to the extreme for what he believed in. I was not going to pass up an opportunity to meet him in person and to listen to what he had to say. I was not disappointed! His many feats are remarkable in themselves – swimming the English Channel, swimming around the Cape of Good Hope, swimming in the Norwegian Fjords.

However, his most outstanding achievement has to be swimming one kilometre at the South Pole. Lewis didn't just jump into the minus 2 degree water and jump out again – perhaps even you and I could do that, if we were crazy enough. No, Lewis needed to make a stronger statement than that, so he swam one kilometre in the middle of the South Pole.

Watching the video of his swim, there were 2 things that I kept thinking to myself. Firstly, this guy is completely nuts and secondly, what drives a person to do this? Why was he willing to do *whatever it takes* in order to alert the world to climate change? What drove him to do this?

Obviously, Lewis realised that simply talking about climate change was one thing, but doing something completely remarkable would hopefully get the world's attention and make us respond in a constructive way. In his case, it worked! It got the attention of the politicians, environmental groups and a number of corporate giants. It also got the attention of little old me! If you have never heard his story, then I strongly urge you to read *Achieving the Impossible* – it will challenge you out of your comfort zone.

Perhaps Lewis Pugh's story has a link with Jesus' story? When God realised that humanity was unresponsive to his overtures of grace and they had drifted into a narcotic spiritual slumber, God decided to do something unique and unthinkable. God sent his son, Jesus, into the world, wooing us back into a relationship with Him. Even when humanity turned their backs on Jesus, God allowed him to be led to the cross, where Jesus demonstrated the depth of his love. In essence, God was willing to do *whatever it takes* to communicate this powerful message with every human on earth…

…. I LOVE YOU! You are precious in my sight.

…..I love you enough to sacrifice my own child in order to win you back.

That is amazing. In fact, it is truly awesome! Who wouldn't want to respond to a God who is willing to do *whatever it takes* to win us back?

Someone who could be viewed as combining Faith with a good cause is Angus Buchan. His influence in the Mighty Men's movement mobilised many men to take their faith seriously and to be more of a godly example in their own families. Angus Buchan has shown us that he is a man who is willing to do *whatever it takes* to honour God and to walk in his ways. Angus would be the first to admit that this has not been an easy road – there have been moments of incredible pain and turmoil, but God has been faithful throughout. And I have no doubt that God will continue to be faithful to us too.

The Bible also holds a powerful example of how one person can be used by God, for the sake of a great cause. This is the life story of Queen Esther. Even though Esther was a Jewish woman, she was chosen as the new Queen of Persia. She had managed to keep her nationality a secret until the day she learned that the entire Jewish community faced genocide. In a moment, she had to face up to her origins and decide to do *whatever it takes* to serve God and save her nation.

On Esther's life, author Karen Jobes adds some amazing insights:

"While her people fast with her, Esther overcomes herself and finds the courage to reveal her identity as a Jew before Xerxes regardless of the consequences. Whether or not she is mindful of the covenant and its promises, her decision to identify with God's people is a decision to risk being an agent through whom God can fulfil those promises."[9]

Did you notice that phrase 'overcome herself'? Esther was not preparing for just any casual meeting with the King – this was the defining moment of her life. This was to be the moment she was going to arrive in the Kings' court, unannounced and then she would proceed to tell her husband she was not who he thought she was – that she was in fact of Jewish descent! You have to get over yourself, if you want to make such a bold move. If she was too hung up on her appearances and her future, she would not have done what she did. She recognised that circumstances had changed to such a degree that she had no option but to do whatever she could to speak out for her people.

Are we willing to risk being agents through whom God can fulfil his purposes? It is a scary thing I know, but we need to sincerely ask ourselves this question.

I vividly remember praying before an evening service, one night in Johannesburg, and feeling quite overwhelmed. I am not a person who cries easily, but in that moment I was overcome with emotion. I felt that I couldn't go out and lead that service – I felt unqualified, scared and nervous. My whole body longed to run out of that vestry and never to return again. However, in the end, I managed to gain composure and all I remember now of that incident, was the overwhelming sense of peace as I preached. I knew I had to rely on God 100% - it needed to be all of him and none of me, otherwise I wasn't going to make it through the sermon. I am grateful that God was so faithful that evening.

Reflecting on Esther's testimony, we note that before she did anything she asked people to fast and pray for her. To me, this was the key in her successful appeal to the King – she had covered the whole situation in prayer and she knew that even if she was killed for her bold appeal, she would be in the hands of God.

King David has many key moments in his life, but somehow I always think back on his defining moment – his confrontation with Goliath. What on earth would possess a shepherd boy to answer the challenge of an angry warrior? Yet, deep within his spirit, David had stored up the memories of how God had delivered him from other dangers – lions, bears and the like. With deep conviction, David offers to fight Goliath – to do *whatever it takes* to bring down the enemy.

There are two clear things in this story: Firstly, David was courageously willing to stand up and fight for his people. Secondly, David knew that God would grant him victory. David could bravely walk into battle, because he was convinced that God was going to do *whatever it takes* to help him. Simple faith, but rock solid!

TIME OF REFLECTION

As we bring this chapter to a close please take the time to reflect on these questions.

1. Is Jesus calling you to be the voice of the marginalised or the oppressed? Are you willing to do *whatever it takes* to fulfil this Godly calling?

2. Looking around at some of the good causes of our generation, is there a particular "champion" who inspires you? What can you learn from their story?

3. Is there a particular issue in your community that you feel Jesus would be committed to be a part of? Do you see any Christ-followers involved in this cause at the moment? If NOT, then what is stopping you from getting involved?

4.   Read Isaiah 1:17. Use these words as a basis for your own prayer.

three

FAME

IS IT REALLY WORTH IT?

"I had the world, and it wasn't nothin'."

- MUHAMMAD ALI

"So the LORD was with Joshua, and his fame spread throughout the land."

- JOSHUA 6:27

As we take a look at the topic of fame, let me start by asking us a question, "how long does fame last?" Do you have any ideas? Does it last 15 minutes, or 3 months, a few years or perhaps even a lifetime? I honestly don't have the answer for you, but it is worth thinking about.

Let us perhaps think about fame in a different way. Do you recognise any of these people?

Owen D. Young,
Pierre Laval,
Hugh S. Johnson,
James F. Byrnes,
Mohammed Mossadegh,
Harlow Curtis.

So how many of the six names did you recognise? My score was a shocking one out of six. The thing is that we should have recognised a few of these people, because according to *Time* magazine, all six of them have been voted as "Man of the Year" at some stage in recent history. This category, according to *Time,* indicates that they had the greatest impact on humanity in that particular year, of all persons living on Earth.

So could it be true that the celebrity of today is all but forgotten tomorrow? After all, fame is just a fleeting moment in the limelight. Today's headline heroes land up being wrapped around a fish and chips meal tomorrow. Perhaps Andy Warhol was indeed right when he predicted that everyone will get their 15 minutes of fame. Some of us are still waiting for our 15 minutes of fame, but perhaps the wait won't be worth it in the end!

In truth, people have been seeking fame for generations. In a world of 7 billion people, it seems that every human being is trying harder and harder to be noticed. People will do *whatever it takes* to be famous, convinced that fame will bring happiness, wealth and abundant life. The tragedy is that it seems the more fame you have the harder it is to live a 'normal' life. The more famous you are, the more the world watches you and the less chance you have to live like the masses in a 'normal' life.

Herein lies the deepest irony – we do *whatever it takes* to be famous and when we are finally noticed, we then try to do *whatever it takes* to get away from the paparazzi and the glitz and glamour. Many famous people often dream of living incognito. Just give them their money and they could quite happily live out their days away from the public limelight.

Greek Mythology has a wonderful way of teaching us a number of vital life lessons. There are many powerful stories in this rich mythology, but the one told of Icarus is most apt in this instance. Icarus and his father Daedalus had been imprisoned on the island of Crete and while they served their time on the island, master craftsman Daedalus, made two pairs of wings out of wax and feathers. Before the two of them fled from the island, Daedalus warned Icarus not to fly too close to the sun or too close to the sea. However Icarus ignored the cautionary advice his father had given him and he allowed the glory of flight to distract him.

Believing that flying had made him almost invincible Icarus soared through the sky, trying to take in his new found freedom and power. Tragically, he ignored his father's advice and he flew too close to the sun. When the heat from the sun's rays melted the wax on the wings, Icarus fell to his death into the sea that now bears his name, the Icarian Sea. People now living near Icaria, will forever have a reminder of how 'fame' and 'power' can destroy your freedom and ultimately your life.

Christian band, Jars of Clay wrote of the myth of Icarus in their song 'Worlds Apart',

"I am the only one to blame for this
Somehow it all ends up the same
Soaring on the wings of selfish pride
I flew too high and like Icarus I collide
With a world I try so hard to leave behind." [10]

One of my concerns with the concept of fame is that it becomes self-serving – it ends up being 'all about me.' It is about my name, my reputation, my desires, my wants and my needs. Of course, some people find fame in unlikely ways and definitely weren't seeking to become famous (Mother Theresa is a prime example of this), but the majority of people who find fame, desire to see their names in neon lights!

In an article he wrote for *Leadership magazine*, Craig Larson tells the following story:
"A friend who lives in a forested area found his home overrun with mice. There were too many to exterminate with traps, so he bought a few boxes

of D-Con and distributed them around the house, including one under his bed. That night he couldn't believe his ears; below him was a feeding frenzy. In the morning he checked the box and found it licked clean. Just to make sure the plan worked he bought and placed another box. Again, the mice went for the flavoured poison like piranha. But the tasty and popular night-time snack did its deadly work. In the days that followed, all was quiet. All of the mice were dead. Just because something is popular doesn't mean it's good for you."

There is so much truth in this story. Just because we live in a society that glorifies fame and popularity does not mean that it is always going to be healthy for us. The lure of fame is deceptive – just like nice looking poison.

"The lure of fame is deceptive - just like nice looking poison"

It may look and taste good for a while, but what is it actually doing to us? Over time the poison of fame, prosperity and success can eat away at our insides in a way that we least expect. If our primary goal in life is to do *whatever it takes* to gain fame, perhaps we need to think again.

We were on holiday in Europe, during the summer of 2011, when the news of Ryan Gigg's shady past caught up with him. I was gutted! Giggs is a Manchester United legend and has always been a hero of mine. I had admired him as a footballer, but also as someone who kept out of the media spotlight. To me and the rest of the world, he seemed to live the perfect 'family life!' But how wrong we all were!

The news of his extra-marital affairs were shocking enough for those of us on the outside, but can you imagine how his family felt? His wife must have felt deeply betrayed and hurt, as too his brother Rhodri. News spread that Ryan had been having an affair with his brother's wife! From a distance it seemed the perfect world, filled with perfect people. However, that illusion was shattered by all the media revelations.

The same story unfolded with golfing legend Tiger Woods. He was seemingly happily married to beautiful Erin Nordegren, but their fairy-tale exploded one dark night. In an instant the whole world got to discover what a few insiders knew all along. Tiger had been unfaithful many times. As much as he tried to cover it up, the truth came out – as it always does. As someone once said, 'what happens in the dark will be revealed in the light.'

Tiger Wood's golf career took a major nose dive in the wake of these revelations and before long he dropped to below 50th in the world. We all know that he is a much better golfer than that, but for someone who once seemed infallible, everything crumbled around him.

We understand that Tiger's father spent hours and hours teaching him golf, as a child. It was a *whatever it takes* approach to sport. The time they spent together not only allowed them to share a unique bond, but it definitely paid off on the golf courses of the world. You can't win Major golf tournaments with no skill and no practise. But, I am still wondering whether that 'whatever it takes' approach didn't somehow heap too much pressure onto a young child. What do you think?

Are the words of Ezekiel too harsh in this case, or does he have a valid point? Have we prostituted ourselves in an attempt to appease our desire for fame?

"'But you trusted in your beauty and used your fame to become a prostitute. You lavished your favours on anyone who passed by and your beauty became his" (Ezekiel 16:15).

It surprises me that people are willing to do all they can to gain fame, sporting success, financial gain and material wealth – yet, tragically, when it comes to the important things in life, there seems to be a lack of desire, willpower, and energy to fight for these things. Friendship, family relationships, and faith are for me the key things in life. If we don't have these three then I honestly feel we are poorer for it.

Fame and legacy often go hand in hand. Famous families want to ensure that their wealth and name are passed onto the next generations and they are willing to go to great lengths to ensure this. In ancient Rome adoption was a common way of ensuring leadership succession. In fact, when emperors and leaders realised that their next of kin were a threat or not up to the task, they readily adopted someone to be their heirs. Augustus Caesar was adopted by his great-uncle, Julius Caesar and a number of other famous emperors were adopted by distant family or acquaintances. These included Tiberius, Trajan, and Hadrian. [11]

It should not surprise us that secular leaders are willing to do *whatever it takes* to maintain their stranglehold on a country or people. The continent of Africa has a number of similar stories: Idi Amin, Robert Mugabe and Muammar Gaddafi are but three clear examples – they have all been willing to do *whatever it takes* to remain in power. The same was true of the biblical kings. King Saul, the first king of the nation of Israel, was so threatened by the young David, that he tried to kill him a number of times. He realised that people were starting to favour a new hero and he felt threatened and insecure. He was willing to do all he could to dispose of the young upstart.

It may seem strange to speak about War in a chapter on fame, but let me explain. Visiting the battlefields of the Somme, in Northern France is a deeply moving experience. Every monument and graveyard is filled with stories of sorrow and pain. The endless rows of white crosses, amidst neatly manicured green grass, left me feeling drained - completely emotionally drained. I asked myself,

How many families around the world wept bitter tears when the news of death filtered home?

How many broken hearts never mended?

How many parents, siblings, friends, and communities spent days in loneliness, hoping that the nightmare would end and their sons would walk through the door?

War is a classic example of *whatever it takes* gone wrong. On a scale of 1 to 10, the greed, power and insanity of war must rank as a 15! It is the best example of how evil decisions, taken by some people, can multiply and drastically impact the lives of millions of people. History reveals that the Battles of the Somme, were nothing new – people have been trying to conquer and rule over each other since Cain and Abel's fight. *Whatever it takes* with selfish motives always ends in disaster. War may bring recognition to a select few – your Adolf Hitler's, Winston Churchill's, Dwight Eisenhower's, but for untold millions it has only brought grief and pain.

The television series *Prisonbreak* was a blockbuster success. Michael Schofield (Wentworth Miller) plays the younger brother who gets arrested so that he can break his brother Lincoln out of Fox River State Penitentiary. I never realised I could get so caught up in a drama about Prison life – the series was addictive.

I also never realised I would end up rooting for a few of the 'good' prisoners to escape from the 'bad' cops. Anyway, personal preferences aside, this Series reminded me of the incredible desire of one man to do *whatever it takes* to rescue his brother. Wentworth put himself through physical pain (anyone who tattoos the blue prints of the entire prison on his body is crazy), and great humiliation, in choosing to go to prison, willingly surrendering to those in authority. He knew the risks of not getting out of prison again, but he felt they were worth the risk.

This is a prime example of the modern media giving us a picture of God's sacrificial love. I know that the makers of Prisonbreak had no desire to share the gospel through their production, but for me, it is unmistakably clear. Jesus lay down his life for us – he did *whatever it takes,* so that we could be freed from our prison of sin and death. He had to come into our world in order to release us for the next. Michael Schofield never wanted any recognition for his sacrificial act. Jesus never sought fame either. Yet, as Jesus' act of love spread around the world, recognition followed. It is true that the name of Jesus is the most well-known around the globe today. It is sad that recognition doesn't always equate to following though!

Just like thousands of children around the globe I was gripped every year by the Wimbledon tennis tournament. I remember rushing outside, after watching a game on television, to hit a tennis ball against our metal garage door (which made a wonderful sound every time I hit it). Our poor neighbours must have hated the two weeks of Wimbledon, because it always coincided with our mid-year holidays, so I had lots of time to practise my tennis shots.

I had hopes of one day playing on Centre court and lifting the crown after a hard fought match against my nearest rival. I even tried to dress up for the occasion – I tried the bandana like Bjorn Borg and it seemed to improve my shots somewhat (at least I thought so in my mind). However, the sad reality was that a month after Wimbledon had finished, I had also packed it in. I had lived a 'dream' for a few weeks, made a few shots against the garage door, but realised that I didn't want it enough. I was not prepared to do *whatever it takes* to reach my wishful goal.

How many Christians do you know who are like this? They committed their lives to the Lord one evening – raised their hands in the back of a church or came forward at a concert – but have drifted back into their normal lives. Their commitment to Christ was not actually with their 'lives' it was just for a few weeks. Their decision to follow Christ was like a flash of flame that got put out by the pressures of life. Perhaps they too realised that they didn't have what it takes to be a Christ-follower. The cost seemed too great.

Following Jesus is tough. When I surrendered my life to Jesus at 16 years of age, no one bothered to tell me that this would be the hardest thing I would ever do. Joyous, exhilarating and awesome, but also incredibly tough! There are days when I am keen to bail out, but deep inside I know that I want to be a Christ-follower through the good and bad.

Francesco Bernardone had a life changing experience in 1223. Climbing to the top of Mount La Verna to flee from the demanding crowds, Francesco was at breaking point. He was dispirited, exhausted and emotionally empty. The forty days that he spent on the mountain changed his life forever. It is said that genuine stigmata marks presented themselves on his body in the exact same places that Jesus was wounded – feet, side and hands. This experience proved to be a catalyst in Francesco's life and shaped the future of Franciscan spirituality for hundreds of years to come. Perhaps you would know him as St. Francis of Assisi.

But, things were not always like this for St Francis. Richard Foster, in

Longing for God, writes, "Francesco had to break free from his fascination with himself before God could use him in a meaningful way....up until he was twenty-four, he wasted his life in a pampered, self-indulgent lifestyle shielded from the harsh realities of everyday life."[12]

His 'first' conversion came in 1205, when he realised that a life of wealth and fame was meaningless. Taking Jesus at his word, Francesco 'denied himself' and left his previous life behind. The world has been forever marked by his decision to do *whatever it takes.* Fame and fortune has nothing on surrendering your life to Christ.

The Bible is not against fame per se. It recognises that certain people will discover fame and honour as they live godly lives. Just look at a few of these verses:

- **1 Chronicles 14:17** - So David's fame spread throughout every land, and the LORD made all the nations fear him.

- **Joshua 6:27** - So the LORD was with Joshua, and his fame spread throughout the land.

Even in our contemporary society well known Christian leaders, like Bill Hybels, Rick Warren, John Ortberg, Andy Stanley and Louis Giglio, have not deliberately gone seeking fame. They have honoured God with their ministries and lives. People have noticed their gifting and they are now recognised names in Christian circles. Their responsibility is even greater now that they are 'famous.'

In the end, it is only God who truly deserves the acclaim and recognition. We should honour God with the words of Habakkuk:
"LORD, I have heard of your fame; I stand in awe of your deeds, O LORD.

Renew them in our day, in our time make them known; in wrath remember mercy." - Habakkuk 3:2

Perhaps it is fitting to allow Thomas a Kempis the last word on this topic. He is one of my favourite Christian mystics and epitomises someone who rejected fame and instead chose to live a simple life.

"We are not naturally inclined
To bear the Cross,
To love the Cross,
To discipline our bodies,
To run away from honours,
To suffer reproach willingly,
To disregard ourselves and to wish to be disregarded,
To endure all trouble and loss
To desire no prosperity in the world.
If you try to accomplish these things yourself you will fail.
But if you trust the Lord, you will receive divine strength,
And you will be able to withstand the world..."

TIME OF REFLECTION

1. Do you look up to someone who is considered to be famous? Who is that person and what about their life inspires you?

2. Are you content to follow Christ even if there is no glamour or recognition from others? Why or why not?

3. What would you most want to be remembered for?

4. What are your thoughts on Deuteronomy 26:19? – "He has declared that he will set you in praise, fame and honour high above all the nations he has made and that you will be a people holy to the LORD your God, as he promised."

four

FORTUNE

THE MIRAGE AT THE END OF THE RAINBOW

"Jesus asks for everything. But we try to give Him less."

- FRANCIS CHAN

"I will give you honour and praise among all the peoples of the earth when I restore your fortunes before your very eyes," says the LORD."

- ZEPHANIAH 3:20

Every year *Forbes* Magazine produces a Rich List. Often this list includes the wealthy people that we all know - Warren Buffet, Bill Gates, Richard Branson and others. However, every year new names appear on this list – people who have achieved a lot in the past 12 months and whose net worth has launched them into the top 100. I think that it goes without saying, that having your name on this list is very prestigious and it is a sure way to be noticed by everyone.

Recently, *Forbes* website claimed that over 1645 people globally, are now Billionaires. I had a quick look at the website and I was fascinated by the lists of people and their net worth. It was like entering into another world. You and I may be tempted to take a look at the names on this list and immediately think to ourselves, 'these people have made it!' And with a Billion dollars in your bank account, it's hard not to think that!

Yet, what we don't often see is how much these people have had to sacrifice in order to reach the top of this list. History is littered with rich people who have done *whatever it takes* in order to attain wealth, power and prestige. This accolade has usually come at a great cost to family, friends and other people. Having a *whatever it takes* attitude towards gaining a fortune can be totally detrimental in the long run. It takes a grounded person not to allow your money to rule your life. Jesus says it best when he warns,

"What good is it to gain the whole world and yet forfeit your soul?" (Mark 8:36).

Author and Pastor, Greg Laurie makes an interesting observation on how money is handled in the Scriptures. He says, "it is worth noting that money is such an important topic in the Bible that it is the main subject of nearly half of the parables Jesus told. In addition, one in every seven verses in the New Testament deals with this topic. The Bible offers 500 verses on prayer, fewer than 500 verses on faith, and more than 2,000 verses on money."

It is certain that Jesus spoke clearly on the topic of wealth, money and treasures, because he believed that there was a profound connection between our spiritual health and the way we handle our finances. Our attitude towards riches and doing *whatever it takes* to gain our fortune could have consequences for our spiritual well-being.

Perhaps one of the most profound things I have read on this issue comes from A. W. Tozer. The following illustration will always remind me of how easy it is to lose focus and to allow money to come between myself and Jesus:

> "Money often comes between men and God. Someone has said that you can take two small ten-cent pieces, just two dimes, and shut out the view of a panoramic landscape. Go to the mountains and just hold two coins closely in front of your eyes--the mountains are still there, but you cannot see them at all because there is a dime shutting off the vision in each eye."[13]

Modern television has been drastically changed by the advent of 'Reality TV'. Programmes such as *Survivor*, *The Apprentice*, *Idols*, *Celebrity Chef* and many others, keep us interested on a weekly basis. It is a little disturbing how quickly we water-down our norms and principles, in favour of our chosen contestant. Take for example, *Survivor*. A player on *Survivor* can lie, cheat and steal, all in the name of the game, and we will still root for them in the end, even though we chastise our kids when we see them do the same thing.

We justify the actions of the contestants by arguing that 'it's about playing the game!' However, these Reality TV shows are not too far from the reality of everyday life. We are surrounded by a culture that urges us to do *whatever it takes* to get what we want. We are lulled into a false belief that 'we deserve it' or 'everyone's doing it', so why not me?

I am not convinced that this is helpful for our society and neither is it God's desire for our lives. Through the words of the apostle Paul, Eugene Peterson reminds us that we are called to live in a different way:

"The world is unprincipled. It is dog-eat-dog out there! The world doesn't fight fair. But we don't live or fight our battles that way – never have and never will. The tools of our trade aren't for marketing or manipulation, but they are for demolishing that entire massively corrupt culture. We use our powerful God – tools for smashing warped philosophies, tearing down barriers erected against the truth of God..."

In the Methodist tradition we host an annual covenant service, usually in the beginning of a new year. John Wesley held the first Covenant service on Monday 11 August 1755, at a French church at Spitalfields in London. The service was designed as a way of getting Christians to renew their commitment to Jesus Christ. The words for this prayer were originally inspired by Richard Alleine and were then adapted by John Wesley.

The Covenant prayer is a *whatever it takes* kind of prayer. This is why at our church we never force people to pray the prayer without understanding what they are actually saying. Instead, we ask people to reflect on the words for a week beforehand. If they feel ready to recommit themselves to following the Jesus Way, then they come the following Sunday, ready to pray the prayer.

These are the modern words of our Covenant Prayer:
I am no longer my own, but yours.
Put me to what you will, rank me with whom you will;
put me to doing, put me to suffering;
let me be employed for you, or laid aside for you,
exalted for you, or brought low for you;
let me be full,
let me be empty,
let me have all things,
let me have nothing:
I freely and wholeheartedly yield all things
to your pleasure and disposal.
And now, glorious and blessed God,
Father, Son and Holy Spirit,
you are mine and I am yours. So be it.
And the covenant now made on earth, let it be ratified in heaven.
Amen.

Do you see what I mean? It is not an easy prayer to pray, is it? In a world which encourages us to pray for fortune, blessing and privilege, this prayer urges us to ask for something different. The covenant prayer recognises that we are not our own anymore, but that we are under the Lordship of

Jesus Christ. And if Christ wants us to have "all things" then he will make that possible, but if God requires that for a time I have "nothing" then I need to be assured that he still loves me. My bank balance is not a sign of God's love for me and not for you either.

I heard a story once of a minister who had just prayed this covenant prayer with his congregation. When he got home, he saw that this house had burnt to the ground, destroying all his earthly possessions. Needless to say he was heart-broken by what he saw, but he was still able to reflect on God's mercy in protecting his family, who had been at church with him. He responded by saying, "It is obvious that for this time, my heavenly father would prefer that I have nothing, but I will trust in his provision for tomorrow." Wow, what a statement of faith. I long to have the kind of trust in God that this minister had.

There is another prayer that I would like to mention at this point – it comes from the scriptures. It is prayed by a man considered to be more distinguished than his brothers. Do you have a clue who he is? No, it is not Joseph, nor David. It is a man named Jabez. To be honest, I had never read of his name until Dr Bruce Wilkinson's book *The Prayer of Jabez* became an international best seller. We know very little of his life and we have no evidence of any heroic act that he performed, yet when we analyse Jabez's prayer we can see what kind of man he was. He was a man willing to pray the big prayers and I am convinced he was willing to do *whatever it takes* to honour God. This is his prayer:

> "Oh, that you would bless me indeed, and enlarge my territory, that your hand would be with me, and that you would keep me from evil, that I may not cause pain." So God granted him what he requested (1 Chronicles 4:10)

This prayer is quite different from the Covenant prayer, as it does ask for blessing and a larger territory, but Jabez ends the request on a sobering note. He does not want to be the cause of pain to anyone and so his prayer is filled with perspective. Although he feels at liberty to ask God for anything, he realises that it may change his life completely and he doesn't want to allow his 'gain' to harm others.

I mention the story of Jabez, because I don't want you to misunderstand me. I am not saying that Christians can't be wealthy or that we shouldn't be entrusted with great wealth. On the contrary, almost every Christian community wouldn't exist if it weren't for the generosity of their members. Some of these people would definitely be considered 'wealthy', but they have used their 'treasures' to fund projects and mission in the community.

If you happen to be a person who has significant material possessions and 'fortune' at the moment, I invite you to share your blessings with others. Perhaps God has brought you to this point in your life, so that you are able to be a financial support to the Church and to those in need. Don't feel guilty about what God has entrusted into your care. I encourage you to be a good steward of these gifts and to see what God can do through your generosity.

"If we make our sole aim in life to become 'Rich', then we may be greatly disappointed along the way."

If we make our sole aim in life to become 'Rich', then we may be greatly disappointed along the way. King Solomon has to be one of the richest kings ever to have lived. He amassed fortune and fame, way beyond even the Forbes Rich List, yet in the end, he still believed that something was not right in his life – he felt that something was missing.

Let's pause for a second.

I want to clearly drive this point home and I hope you don't miss what I am saying. If you find yourself in the privileged position of having made your fortune or having lots of resources at your disposal please DO NOT feel guilty about this. I would rather urge you to consider why God has blessed you with so much and to ask how you can be a blessing to others.

It is not helpful to 'guilt' anyone into doing something. What is more productive is when we take an honest look at our material comforts and then seek to be agents of God's love to others. I like the image of holding onto our material possessions 'loosely'. If we grab onto them, believing that they are our salvation, then we open ourselves up for major disappointment.

Many of us may be fooled into thinking that money is security, but in writing to Timothy, Paul warns that it can be just the opposite, "Those who want to get rich fall into temptation and a trap and into many foolish and harmful desires that plunge people into ruin and destruction" (1 Timothy 6:9).

A few years ago, columnist Jim Bishop reported on what happened to people who had won the US state lottery. He mentions one person in particular, Rosa Grayson of Washington. When Rosa won the lottery she won the right to receive $400 (R 5000) a week, for the rest of her life. Wow, that would seem like an incredible gift, but it proved to be otherwise. Rosa now hides in her apartment and is afraid to venture out. She claims that for the first time in her life, she is nervous of other people. She has found that everyone tries to get some money from her and this has made her feel used and miserable.

The *Daily Walk* tells a similar story – this time of John G. Wendel and his sisters, who were some of the most miserly people of all time. Their lives too were wrecked by fortune. Although they had received a huge inheritance from their parents, they spent very little of it and did all they could to keep their wealth for themselves. John was able to influence five of his six sisters never to marry, and they lived in the same house in New York City for 50 years. When the last sister died in 1931, her estate was valued at more than $100 million. Her only dress was one that she had made herself, and she had worn it for 25 years.

The Wendels had such a compulsion to hold on to their possessions that they lived like paupers. Even worse, they were like the kind of person Jesus referred to "who lays up treasure for himself, and is not rich toward God" (Luke 12:21). All of these people had hoped and prayed for sudden wealth – a miracle to make their lives better. And they all had their prayers answered, but at a great cost.

In speaking of the ancient Israelites, John Oswalt could easily be speaking about someone in our modern times: "If the goal of one's life is to take care of oneself, then serving one's own appetites and perverting justice in order to do so are as logical as any mathematics."[14] There was clearly a time when God's children took their eyes off Jehovah and began to look for other treasures. Soon their dependence on God, moved to a dependence on self and material wealth. This spelt the beginning of the end for the Israelites.

In Isaiah 5:1-30, the prophet speaks about a certain Vineyard. He warns the nation about their present lifestyle, using 5 woes, to get their attention. If you read through these verses you will see he speaks about issues that still impact us in the twenty-first century:

- greed (v.8),
- self-indulgence (v.11-17),
- cynicism (v.18-19),
- moral perversion (v.20-21)
- social injustice (v.22-24).

In every generation it seems that people strive to live for themselves. The *whatever it takes* attitude is perverted to mean – let me do this for myself. Tough luck to the rest of you! But is this the way that Christians are called to live? I am not so sure. Solomon warns us, "a fortune made by a lying tongue is a fleeting vapour and a deadly snare" (Proverbs 21:6).

It is not by accident that Isaiah then leads us into the well-known chapter 6, which deals with a new kind of attitude – which involves serving God. Isaiah had an amazing vision of God and in that moment he realised how small he was in the presence of the Almighty God. Isaiah also came to a deep knowledge of his unworthiness and his sin. In an act of mercy and forgiveness an angel touches his lips with a burning coal and pronounces that his sins are forgiven. It is as if the Lord wants to set Isaiah apart from the rest of the Israelites – God cleanses him from the lifestyle that was pervading his community.

Finally God gets to the nitty-gritty. He asks the Israelites a challenging question,

"Whom should I send as a messenger to my people. Who will go for us?" (v8, NLT)

And it is Isaiah who courageously steps forward and states, *"Lord I'll go, send me."*

Our Christian faith is under attack. Our beliefs and principles are being hijacked right from right under our noses and we are blissfully unaware what is happening. The world's standards of 'pleasure at all costs', 'comfort first', 'look after yourself' and 'no more rules' have crept into our churches and homes at an alarming rate. Reflecting on the story of Isaiah John Oswalt writes:

> "Studies show that Christian teenagers are almost as likely to cheat as are non-Christians, so more than half of them think that there are no absolute moral standards. Divorces among evangelicals now exceed the national norm. What has happened? We are slowly losing our grip on the idea that there is a Creator whose character is absolutely consistent and who has created human beings in his image. We are losing the idea that this Creator has built into his universe certain spiritual principles that are as unchanging as any of the natural principles." [15]

What will it take for us to stem the tide? It may just mean that you and I have to stand up and be counted. We may need to do *whatever it takes* to bring the power of God back into our homes, schools, work environments and dare I say it, even into our Churches!

Let me also add that the Church is not immune from the allure of 'fortune' and 'wealth'. In a world that also advocates the *whatever it takes* methodology, Christian leaders can often choose the wrong path. Sadly, many Christians have got caught up in ungodly things. As David Nystrom comments, "Clergy stumble too. Some are driven by a desire for money …. other clergy simply crave power." This is why I think it is always advisable to have Christian friends who can keep us accountable in our lifestyle choices.

During a recent sermon series on 1 Peter, it struck me again how Christ called the early Church to suffer with him. When people surrendered their lives to Jesus, they expected suffering to be part of the package deal. This is something we have largely forgotten in the Western Church, or at least we have failed to mention to our people.

As a young Christian, I read Charles Sheldon's classic, *In His Steps.* I was greatly moved by his novel and tried to live by the 'what would Jesus do' principal that emerged from his book. However, it was only recently, when I was re-reading 1 Peter 2:21, that I realised that Peter was speaking about something more challenging.

> "To this you were called, because Christ suffered for you, leaving you an example, that you should follow in his steps."

It is easier to call us to follow Christ's example of love, mercy, forgiveness and grace (well, sort of). But what Peter is challenging the early Christians to remember is that Jesus left us an example of suffering. We are called to follow in those footsteps – the path of suffering. I wonder how many of us are willing to wear the 'What would Jesus do' bracelets now? We find it easier to ask God for the love and grace part, but don't expect us to suffer!

There is a short verse in Luke's gospel that makes me feel uncomfortable. It reads, "In the same way, any of you who does not give up everything he has cannot be my disciple' (Luke 14:33). What does Jesus mean by 'everything'? How do we even begin to do that?

I found part of an answer by reading *The Irresistible Revolution* by Shane Claiborne. Shane is not an ordinary kind of guy. His commitment and faith in Jesus takes him into places that few Christians want to go. He is the leading figure in what is being described as the New Monasticism movement. He founded a community in Philadelphia, called *The Simple*

Way. This faith community in the inner city of Philadelphia, has helped to create and connect radical faith communities around the globe. He passionately explores issues like social justice, peace-making and following Jesus.

It wasn't always like this for Shane though. He grew up in a community that was fairly affluent. He got a good education, attending good schools and university. He even did an internship at one of America's Mega-Churches, but he always felt that something was missing. It was while he served alongside Mother Theresa, on the streets of Calcutta, that Shane really decided to do *whatever it takes* for the Gospel. This led him to make some drastic changes in his lifestyle and the way he understood Christianity. Of course his ideology isn't embraced by all Christians, but the way he lives his life is deeply challenging to a community obsessed with money. When asked about the kind of God he believed in, Shane replied, "a God who is saving some of us from the ghettos of poverty, and some of us from the ghettos of wealth."

The history of Christianity reminds us that whenever the Church focused too much on power and money, she lost her way. Leaders and Clergy become corrupt and the message of the Gospel became diluted in the cesspools of greed. One of the reactions to this was Monasticism. It was a radical response to the state of the Church and as a result thousands of Christians abandoned everything to live in the desert of communities of faith. In renouncing earthly treasures, these men and women, sought a different way of life. They were willing to do *whatever it takes* to reclaim the purity of their faith. As C.S. Lewis remarks, "Christians who did the most for the present world were precisely those who thought most of the next. It is since Christians have ceased to think of the other world that we have become ineffective in this."

I get so excited when I discover a hidden treasure while reading. Today,

I was reading through a totally unrelated book, when I stumbled across the name of Edgar Guest. Something intrigued me about this man and so I Googled his poems. I was amazed to discover that he wrote over 11000 poems in his lifetime – that is truly remarkable. What is equally brilliant is that one of his poems focuses on what is important in our lives. I believe his poem *All that Matters* is a fitting way to end this chapter.

When all that matters shall be written down
And the long record of our years is told,
Where shame, like flesh, must perish and grow cold;
When the tomb closes on our fair renown
And priest and layman, sage and motleyed clown
Must quit the places which they dearly hold,
What to our credit shall we find enscrolled?
And what shall be the jewels of our crown?
 I fancy we shall hear to our surprise
Some little deeds of kindness, long forgot,
Telling our glory, and the brave and wise
Deeds which we boasted often, mentioned not.
God gave us life not just to buy and sell,
And all that matters is to live it well. [16]

As we end our discussion on doing *whatever it takes* to gain fortune and financial security, I invite you to spend a few minutes reflecting on these thoughts.

TIME OF REFLECTION

1. "Money will buy a bed but not sleep;
    books but not brains;
    food but not appetite;
    finery but not beauty;
    a house but not a home;
    medicine but not health;
    luxuries but not culture;
    amusements but not happiness;
    religion but not salvation;
    a passport to everywhere but heaven."[17]

What strikes you as you read this poem?

2. If you would like to know what Jesus had to say about wealth and fortune, spend some time reading through the gospels or do a search on the internet. Your results may surprise you.

3. In his great book, *Whose life is it anyway*, Neil Hood writes "few things test a person's spirituality more accurately than the way he or she uses money." How does this quote make you feel?

---

4.   If you find yourself in the fortunate position of being 'wealthy', don't allow your guilt to stop you from being generous. Use what you have been given to further God's work and to bless others.

five

FORGIVENESS

IS IT POSSIBLE TO FORGIVE OTHERS?

"At the heart of the Universe is God's desire to give and to forgive."

- RICHARD FOSTER

"Be kind and compassionate to one another, forgiving each other, just as in Christ God forgave you."

- EPHESIANS 4:32

Corrie Ten Boom's family rescued many Jews during the Second World War. They sheltered them in their Dutch home, at great cost to themselves. One day their secret was discovered, and so Corrie and her father, brother Willem, sisters Betsie and Nollie, were all sent to various concentration camps. Corrie's father only survived for a few days, but she had the nightmare of watching her sister Betsie being beaten to death by the SS guards.

After the war, Corrie felt called to spread God's message of love and forgiveness all over the world. She had been speaking at a particular church in Munich when a man approached her after the service. She immediately recognised him as one of the SS guards who had beaten and abused Betsie. As he stretched out his hand to shake hers, the former guard agreed that it is wonderful to know that God forgives all our sins.

In that moment, Corrie didn't want to reach out and shake his hand, but by the grace of God she found the strength to shake his hand. She recalls that as she did this God's love flooded into her inner being and she began to feel God's love for this man.

People marvel at this story. Most of us can't imagine ourselves loving and forgiving in this manner – it seems too hard for us. Sometimes I wonder what I would have done. My human instinct is to think that I probably would have punched him in the face while his hand was outstretched (sorry, that's not very spiritual, I know). Forgiveness is tough. Corrie Ten Boom has shown me an example of Christ's love and mercy – Jesus was prepared to do *whatever it takes* to forgive me, so now I need to respond in a similar way. Pray for me as I wrestle with this – I will pray for you too!

When I don't feel strong, that's when I know that God is nearest to me. When I feel wobbly, I sense God drawing nearer to me. It's like when we taught our kids to ride their bicycles. When they were finding the balancing tricky, we ran alongside them and tried to catch them if they fell over. However as they got more and more confident, we were able to let them go. Soon they were able to ride by themselves, under our watchful eye, of course. I picture God doing the same with me. I am willing to do all I can to be a Christ-follower, but I understand that I am always under the careful and loving eye of my God. It's my decision to follow Jesus, but he has not left me to my own devices.

As a South African I am grateful for the forgiveness displayed by Nelson Mandela. After being imprisoned for 27 years, one would have enough reason to hate others, but Madiba chose the harder road of forgiveness. In the movie *Invictus* (which tells the story of the 1995 Rugby World Cup) there is a part where Mandela is speaking to a security guard, who is struggling with Madiba's gracious nature. Mandela says to him, "The time for forgiveness is now!"

On the 5th December 2013 we held a memorial service for Nelson Mandela. During the service it struck me how differently my life could have turned out, if he had allowed hatred to cloud his leadership. For me, Madiba chose to do *whatever it takes* on two fronts: he was prepared to die for freedom and democracy, but he was also prepared to live with an attitude of forgiveness. He embodied the words of Alan Paton:

"A great duty falls upon us all, to be the bearers of God's forgiveness, to be the instrument of his love, to be active in compassion" [18]

For me, the most profound story of forgiveness in the Old Testament is that of Joseph. You may remember his story. Sold into slavery by his jealous brothers, he ends up a prisoner in Egypt. Serving in Potiphar's palace, he is falsely accused of sexual harassment and is thrown into prison. While in prison, he meets Pharaoh's cup-bearer and baker, who are greatly disturbed by their dreams. Joseph interprets their dreams for them, and both dreams come true. The baker is executed, and the cup-bearer is released from prison, but everyone forgets the young man who interprets dreams.

Two years pass by, when Pharaoh is disturbed by his dreams. Suddenly the cup-bearer remembers Joseph and tells Pharaoh all about his gift. Joseph correctly interprets his dreams and Pharaoh is highly impressed with him. Eventually he is appointed as the 2nd in command of the entire land.

Up to this point in his life enough "stuff" had happened to Joseph to give him every reason to be bitter and to harbour unforgiveness in his heart. Wouldn't you agree? But let's fast forward to the part where Joseph reveals his identity to his brothers. One can see the huge emotional strain it was on him – he wept as he told them who he was. It wasn't only because he was happy to see them, but I believe because of the years of emotional baggage he had had to carry. I am sure that he had planned the scenario through in his mind a number of times – "How would I react if I meet my brothers again?" Perhaps his anger stirred up deeply inside him – forgiveness was not going to be easy.

William Barclay adds some wisdom to this particular point:

"There is one eternal principal which will be valid as long as the world lasts. The principle is - Forgiveness is a costly thing. Human forgiveness is costly. A son or a daughter may go wrong; a father or a mother may forgive; but that forgiveness has brought tears ... There was a price of a broken heart to pay. Divine forgiveness is costly. God is love, but God is holiness. Sin must have its punishment or the very structure of life disintegrates. And God alone can pay the terrible price that is necessary before men can be forgiven. Forgiveness is never a case of saying: "It's all right; it doesn't matter." Forgiveness is the most costly thing in the world."[19]

Of course, Joseph's story reminds us of God's forgiveness for us. For this we need to turn to Jesus when He was speaking from the cross. Luke's Gospel records his words in a passage from Luke 23:32-39. It may be helpful to find a Bible and to turn to these verses now.

I still find it incredible that despite all that the soldiers, the Pharisees, the crowds and Judas did to Jesus, He hardly uttered a word in His own defence. Most of us, would have been spitting mad and would have let fly with an array of choice words. Yet, when Jesus decides to open His mouth to speak anything - the words He chooses are the words of a prayer:

"Father, Forgive them, for they know not what they do."
Isn't it amazing that Jesus prays a prayer at this time. Why didn't He rather plead with the legions of angels to come and rescue Him? Why didn't He call lightning to fall from the sky and singe the soldiers? Why didn't He ask the Father to darken the sky and allow the disciples the chance to rescue Jesus? But no, instead He prays for forgiveness.

He prays for Peter's cowardice.

He prays for Judas' betrayal.

He prays for Pilate's compromise.

He prays for the Pharisees' hypocrisy.

He prays for the soldier's violence.

He prays for the crowd's hatred.

He prays for the forgiveness I so desperately need!

If we analysed Jesus' three word prayer *(Father Forgive Them)* for a moment, we see that in a sense, he is praying for forgiveness in these two areas:

i.   Our **Actions**

ii.   Our **Words**

It was the <u>actions</u> of the people that would have hurt Jesus most, especially in a physical sense. However, it was also the <u>words</u> of these people that would have been extremely painful. These would have been words, like:

- "Crucify Him!"
- "He Saved Others, let him save himself!"
- "If you are the King of the Jews, save yourself."
- "Save us too!"

This is such an important thing for us to grasp too, because when we approach Jesus for the forgiveness of our sins, it is often for the very same reasons. Through the working of the Holy Spirit, I realise that through my actions I hurt other people and this in turn offends Jesus. But I also need to ask for forgiveness when my words have cut others deeply. When I have spoken out of turn or gossiped maliciously or in some other way. We also need to know that Jesus forgives us for our ACTIONS and our WORDS.

You see when it comes to my sins there are many things that I can try regarding these sins. I can try and make up for the wrongs I have caused. I can try and counterbalance them with good works. We can say sorry for them. We can weep over them. We can be filled with regret over them. We can do all of these things, but the one thing I can't do, is pronounce 'FORGIVENESS' over my own sins. Only God can do that! And so, Jesus asks his dad to forgive my sins!

Why did Jesus pray this prayer *"Father, forgive them?"*

Because, He was taking our sin upon himself at that time – every action and word that had been uttered and every sin committed, Jesus was paying the price for them, in that moment. Forgive them Lord, because I am taking their punishment. It is being paid for!

But, Jesus wasn't saying, "Lord, ignore what they've done!" In a way, he was saying, "Father, don't let your mercy stop – let it still flow towards these people, if they repent and see the error of their way." In other words, *'they did not know what they were doing!"*

The words of the Lord's Prayer also reminds us of this:
"Forgive us our debts, as we also have forgiven our debtors." - Matthew 6:12
I know that most of us have no problem begging God to 'forgive our debts, or sins, or trespasses.' We think to ourselves, "I have sinned against you

Lord – please forgive me."

Yet, we often stop half way into verse 12 and ignore the rest of the message. This is one of those tricky passages that suggests we are truly forgiven when we forgive others. It is an expectation that God has of us. It is the only part of the Lord's Prayer where Jesus felt the need to add a little extra onto the end. See what he says in verses 14-15:

*"For if you forgive men when they sin against you, your heavenly Father will also forgive you. **BUT** if you do not forgive men their sins, your Father will not forgive your sins."*

Wow, this doesn't seem fair hey?! Yet, we must note that God is not begrudging us his forgiveness because He is mean and nasty, it is just the way God designed things – I cannot receive LOVE and FORGIVENESS if I am holding onto something else.

If my hands are grasping onto something tightly, I cannot receive anything in return. I usually illustrate this point by getting someone to hold onto something (like a pile of books or something fairly heavy). Then I gently toss them a ball. They either have to watch the ball bounce off their hands or if they want to catch the ball, they have to drop their books. This is what Augustine meant when he said:

"God gives where he finds empty hands."

This was one of the key things in the parable of the unmerciful servant (recorded in Matthew 18:21-35). The forgiveness and grace he received actually made no difference to him in the end, because he was unwilling to let go of the grudges he was holding onto.

I am not, for one second, proclaiming that forgiving others is easy. I am not that naive. But do we think that forgiveness was the easy option for Jesus? When He was dying on the cross and He uttered the words: "Father, forgive them, for they know not what they do," this could not have been easy at all.

As we bring this chapter to a conclusion, let me also offer a few thoughts on what I believe forgiveness is NOT.

a. Forgiveness does not mean that we will cease to hurt – some of our wounds are so deep that it may take years to heal.

"God gives where he finds empty hands "

b. Forgiveness does not mean that we will forget – I think the notion of 'forgiving and forgetting' is a false one. It is more realistic that I choose no longer to use the memory of the incident against others. Let's take Jesus as an example – there is no way that He would have forgotten what people did to him, but when he forgave everyone, he was saying: "No longer will this memory cause a barrier between us."

c. Forgiveness doesn't imply that the other party will recognise that they have offended us. As Sarah Paddison writes, "Sincere forgiveness isn't coloured with expectations that the other person apologize or change."

d. Forgiveness is not pretending that the offence did not really matter. Of course it mattered, but forgiveness is making sure that it no longer controls my behaviour.

I think this issue of forgiveness is well worth practising, because I know we will need to forgive someone in our lifetime and we too will need to ask for forgiveness one day. To refuse to forgive someone is to violate God's nature and character!

I vividly remember struggling to forgive someone in my life. At a point I felt it was just too hard. I had been praying and praying, but it just didn't seem to be working. Eventually I realised that unless I actually said the words, "I forgive you", to that particular person, I was never going to heal. It was as if my own relationship with Christ was being poisoned by the unforgiving spirit I harboured in my heart.

What got me to the point of forgiveness was remembering this challenging quote:

"We will never be able to reproduce any reasonable likeness of Jesus in our hearts and lives as long as we harbour bitterness, unforgiveness and resentment in our hearts". [20]

I found that to be true in my experience and once I found the courage to say "I forgive you" I felt an overwhelming sense of peace in my heart. Eugene Peterson writes, "In prayer there is a connection between what God does and what you do. You can't get forgiveness from God, for instance, without also forgiving others. If you refuse to do your part, you cut yourself off from God's part." [21]

It seems that throughout the history of humanity, people haven't fully comprehended what consequences our sins have on others. But when we have comprehended how much it destroys others, then we have found forgiveness and grace.

If there ever was a man who sought to do *whatever it takes* it was David.

Sadly, a number of his decisions were based on a selfish desire to do things for his own satisfaction. One could argue that he may have done *whatever it takes* to ruin his life and his position as king of Israel. His most shocking decision involved a beautiful young woman named Bathsheba – this is my version of what happened:

He was out on the roof of his palace when he peered over into the neighbour's garden, only to see a stunning women bathing. The sight of a gorgeous naked woman taking a bath was too much for David's hormones. Instead of moving away from the obvious temptation, David sent word to Bathsheba inviting her over to his palace. When the King invites you to his palace you don't really have much room for excuses and so Bathsheba accepted the invitation. David didn't just have a 'coffee morning' in mind and soon he lured Bathsheba into the bedroom. One thing led to another and a few months later she discovered she was pregnant.

As David tried to deny it, he also tried to do everything to clean up his mess, sending Bathsheba's husband Uriah out into the frontline of battle. He hoped that Uriah would be hit by a stray arrow and his plan worked. Bathsheba's husband Uriah died an honourable man, defending the people of Israel, while his wife was pregnant with the King's child.

In a further act of betrayal, David marries Bathsheba, thinking that all will now be well. However, he doesn't count on the prophet Nathan calling him out. Nathan confronts David and makes him comprehend the magnitude of his actions. David is remorseful as he grasps what he has done to his reputation and his relationship with God. We see how he expresses his sin and emotions in a moving song, which we read as Psalm 51.

Have mercy on me, O God,
according to your unfailing love;
according to your great compassion
  blot out my transgressions.
Wash away all my iniquity
  and cleanse me from my sin.

For I know my transgressions,
  and my sin is always before me.
Against you, you only, have I sinned
  and done what is evil in your sight,
so that you are proved right when you speak
  and justified when you judge.

 Surely I was sinful at birth,
  sinful from the time my mother conceived me.
Surely you desire truth in the inner parts;
  you teach me wisdom in the inmost place.

Cleanse me with hyssop, and I will be clean;
  wash me, and I will be whiter than snow.
Let me hear joy and gladness;
  let the bones you have crushed rejoice.
Hide your face from my sins
  and blot out all my iniquity.

Create in me a pure heart, O God,
  and renew a steadfast spirit within me.
Do not cast me from your presence
  or take your Holy Spirit from me.

Whatever it Takes

Restore to me the joy of your salvation
  and grant me a willing spirit, to sustain me.

These words are David's desire for repentance. They are David's way of doing whatever he can to restore his relationship with God.

Forgiveness is not an easy thing to receive nor to grant. It requires a huge amount of humility to ask someone to forgive us, but it also needs 'bucket loads' of love to forgive those who have hurt us.

Apparently when Leonardo Da Vinci was painting *The Last Supper*, he had a massive fight with one of his friends. In anger and malice he made up his mind to draw his friend's face as the portrait of Judas – the one who betrayed Jesus. And so he did this! He then moved on to try and draw the face of Jesus, but no matter how hard he tried, he just kept failing and failing. He was about to give up when he suddenly felt convicted about his painting of his friends face as Judas and so he wiped off his friends face from the canvas.

That night Leonardo Da Vinci had a dream in which he saw the face of Jesus in such a vivid way – he had never seen his face like that before. So in the morning he began to transfer this image from his mind onto the canvas quickly and joyfully. That is the secret to the beauty of the face of Jesus.

To be true Christians, we must first accept Christ's forgiveness of our sins and then we must be willing to forgive others.

TIME OF REFLECTION

To end this chapter I have included two prayers and a question. I hope that these will all be helpful on your journey towards forgiveness.

1. "Father, seeing how freely you have loved me with my imperfections, grant that I may equally love others with theirs. Amen." – **Unknown author**

2. "Lord, remember not only the men and woman of good will, but also those of ill will. But do not remember all of the suffering they have inflicted upon us: Instead remember the fruits we have borne because of this suffering, our fellowship, our loyalty to one another, our humility, our courage, our generosity, the greatness of heart that has grown from this trouble. When our persecutors come to be judged by you, let all of these fruits that we have borne be their forgiveness."- Found in the clothing of a dead child at Ravensbruck concentration camp.

• What does Jesus teach about forgiveness? **Read this** - "If you forgive anyone his sins, they are forgiven; If you do not forgive them, they are not forgiven." (John 20:23). Is this fair?

3. Who is God prompting you to forgive? What are you going to do about it?

"Teach us, good Lord, to serve Thee as Thou deserves; to give and not to count the cost; to fight and not to heed the wounds; to toil and not to ask for rest; to labour and not to ask for any reward, save that of knowing that we do thy will. Through Jesus Christ our Lord." – St Ignatius of Loyola

FAMILY

LIVING WITH THOSE WHO KNOW YOUR DARK SIDE.

"Family quarrels are bitter things. They don't go by any rules. They're not like aches or wounds; they are more like splits in the skin that won't heal because there's not enough material."

- F. SCOTT FITZGERALD

It seems that some people just don't have the will to make things work out. "If you really want to do something, you will find a way – if you don't you will find an excuse."

- JIM ROHN

It surprises me that we are willing to go to incredible lengths to forge successful careers, yet when it comes to putting family and loved ones first we are not willing to show the same level of commitment. Simply put - we are not willing to do *whatever it takes* to preserve and protect the family bond anymore.

Making a tongue-in-cheek comment on the state of many family relationships, Robert Orben writes,

"Who can ever forget Winston Churchill's immortal words:

"We shall fight on the beaches, we shall fight on the landing grounds, we shall fight in the fields and in the streets, we shall fight in the hills."

It sounds exactly like our family vacations!"

Sadly, many families don't just have struggles on vacation - they face troubles all year round. A large number of these family struggles arise out of poor decisions taken by a certain member of the family. The consequences of these decisions often have far reaching implications.

Patrick Morley writes, "Of all the areas that suffer from poor choices, the one area that suffers the most is our relationships. Even though we get into right relationship with God through recommitment, we are not automatically in right relationship with one another. The second most important thing to God is that we get into right relationship with one another." [22]

We are not always ready and willing to put first things first in our family relationships. It seems as if our family commitments fall down the pecking order and no longer hold a priority for us. As C.S. Lewis once remarked, "Put first things first and you will get second things thrown in. Put second things first and you will lose both first and second things." [23]
How true that is!

There is a classic example of a *whatever it takes* family in the first book of the Bible. The amazing story of Jacob and Esau spans numerous chapters in Genesis and it contains all the intricacies of a messy family relationship and would make a brilliant plot for a soap opera.

Like many Israelites, Jacob had been given his name at his birth. During his birth it seemed that he was trying to grab the heel of his twin brother Esau and so the name Jacob, meaning 'someone who grabs the heel' or 'deceiver', seemed perfect for him. From his first breath Jacob seems to live up to his name and he does whatever he can to trick Esau out of his blessing and birth-right.

The issue of favouritism also created tension in this family, ultimately causing major divisions – Isaac favoured Esau and Rebekah favoured Jacob. Despite being the second-born Jacob is prepared to do *whatever it takes* to get the blessing from his Father, and his mother is eager to help her favourite son.

The climax of this story sees Jacob taking food to his father, putting goat skin on his arms and neck (to mimic being hairy like Esau) and wearing Esau's clothes, in order to smell like him. His deception works like a charm and the aging Isaac passes on the family blessing to Jacob. When Esau discovers the deception he is angry and threatens to kill Jacob. Jacob is forced to flee his family home and so through all of his selfish actions Jacob's family is torn apart. One act of greed destroys an entire family! Out of this family mess, Rebekah speaks to Jacob and urges him to run away.

"Flee at once to Laban in Haran... when you brother is no longer angry with you and forgets what you did to him, I'll send word for you to come back from there. WHY SHOULD I LOSE BOTH OF YOU IN ONE DAY?" (Genesis 27:43-45)

Thankfully the story doesn't end at this depressing point. We read how God provides Jacob with opportunities to make things right and so God encounters Jacob at Bethel (Genesis 28) and then later at the Jabbok river (Genesis 32). God desperately tries to get Jacob's attention and Jacob slowly starts to listen.

As the biblical narrative unfolds we see how he begins to get his faith into proper perspective again and this impacts the way that he sees things with Esau. Jacob then has a choice to make and he chooses to do *whatever it takes* to make things right between himself and Esau. He even offers Esau hundreds of animals in exchange for peace and reconciliation.

However, at the same time, God had also been working in Esau's heart and so the story reaches a climax in a moment of reconciliation between the two brothers. This is what it says in Genesis 33:4 - "... Esau ran to meet Jacob and embraced him; he threw his arms around his neck and kissed him."

I realise that we all have the potential to make mistakes, but even the biggest mistakes we have made are not impossible to repair and restore. Bad choices can be rectified when we come to genuine repentance and are willing to make amends.

Of course seeing two brothers like Jacob and Esau fight is nothing new for us - Cain and Abel did it; Joseph and his brothers did it; my three sons do it on a daily basis! History is filled with examples of families that squabble and argue.

Sometimes it ends in complete brokenness. Take the story of brothers, Noel and Liam Gallagher as another example. They are still caught up in the midst of a family feud. The once popular band Oasis topped all the record charts in the UK during the late 1990's, selling 70 million albums, but a mixture of fame, pride, jealousy and unforgiveness has ruined Oasis and the relationship between two brothers. Whether their story will end in up reconciliation, remains to be seen, but it is further proof that families are not immune from selfish personalities and foolish decisions.

I am saddened at how little some people want to fight for their relationships. I come across a number of broken relationships in the community and invariably one party wants to do all they can to make it work and the other just wants to call it quits. I know that this may seem like a generalisation, but I am convinced that more relationships and marriages would survive if both parties were willing to do *whatever it takes* to make things work. The chances of rebuilding a relationship after a personal crisis are much greater when both parties are committed to the process. I realise this is often a humbling and painful journey, but I have personally witnessed marriages thrive when both parties chose to stick things out and do all they could to turn things around.

Sometimes we look at situations in our marriages and relationships and they look impossible – it is as if the odds are stacked against us and no matter how hard we try we will never win. Well, I want to encourage us to remember that we believe in a miraculous God. When the odds of Jesus returning from the grave were zero, God stepped in and changed the shape of religion and faith for forever. God can do the same for your relationships too, if you are willing to walk with him into the unknown.

Can God help us to restore something that seems destroyed and beyond repair?

You bet God can! He staked his son's life on it.

"God can help us restore something that seems broken beyond repair!"

Barbara Johnson is an incredible woman. She has experienced much hardship and tragedy in her life, yet she maintains an amazing belief in Jesus and an infectious hope in life. She has lost 2 sons, both killed in accidents, and journeyed with another son through his struggle with his sexuality. Facing a particular crisis with her son, Larry, she faced losing him forever, as he chose to disown the family. This is Barbara's account of the events:

"Larry did not listen. He hung up in anger, telling us that he was going to change his name and disown us because he never wanted to see us again. Sure enough, a few days later we received the official papers from the court that told us he had done just that. It was early in 1980. We would not hear from Larry for six years. I would go out to speak and share with parents about how to handle pain and someone would ask, "How is your family doing now?"

My standard answer was: "Well, my two sons haven't risen from the dead, and I have a third son who has changed his name, disowned his family, told us he never wants to see us again... But who wants to hear a dreary story like that? I'm here to tell you not to give up hope, particularly when you're in a hopeless situation, because God only gives out the score on a life when the game is over – and the game isn't over YET with my kid."[24]

Wow, what an amazing attitude. What an amazing faith! Barbara has sought to do whatever she can to love her son, even though he didn't want to receive her love. Barbara is the first to admit that she made some mistakes in her reaction to her son's homosexuality, but together they have sought to restore their relationship. Her unconditional love for Larry, drove her to seek ways of rescuing their most precious bond.

When I read this story, I was immediately reminded of Luke's account of the Prodigal son. He too came back sheepishly to the family member he had disowned and hurt (his dad), but it was the act of his loving father that teaches us about the true nature of grace and forgiveness.

Parents are often neurotic and over-protective of their children, but any parent dealing with sick children will openly speak of anxiety, helplessness and quiet desperation. We have had our fair share of sleepless nights, cleaning up vomit, changing bed-sheets, nursing kids with dangerously high temperatures and praying for the morning. I don't consider Kim and I to be panicky parents, but I will openly admit that we are willing to do *whatever it takes* to ensure the well-being of our children. Financial costs, change in work routines, seeking the best advice and so on, are all sacrifices we are more than willing to make.

A few years ago, when our middle son Nathan was still 5 years old, we were happily enjoying a family meal, when he suddenly started choking on a piece of meat. After trying everything we could, we eventually managed to clear his windpipe enough so that he could get some air into his lungs. However, we realised that there was still something blocking his windpipe and he was starting to panic. Without hesitation Kim rushed him to the emergency hospital, while I tried to arrange someone to look after the other 2 children.

Thankfully, our story had a miraculous ending – just as Nathan was being prepped for the anaesthetic and the doctors were getting their 'green gear' on, Nathan coughed violently and the offending piece of meat dislodged by itself. Our relief was tangible and whatever emergency fees we had to pay were nothing in comparison with having Nathan being able to breathe again.

Just reflect for a moment, what would you do to save someone's life? Would you risk your own? I am sure that you would contemplate it. Most parents would certainly do what we did, without much pausing to think of the consequences. Some parents have done even more. Parents have given kidneys, livers and other body parts in order to give their precious kids another chance of survival. My cousin Sam, has just given one of her kidneys to her husband Graham – it was his final chance at a healthy life and she was willing to do all she could for him!

As much as this encounter reminded us of how precious our children are, I couldn't help remembering the movie *John Q*. In this movie a father can't do *whatever it takes* to save his child because they lacked the financial resources. So, John has to rush his sick child to hospital, but because they don't have any medical insurance, the hospital refuses to accept him. His son desperately needs a heart transplant, but he is unable to get one.

The movie then focuses on how John takes the situation into his own hands. In doing *whatever it takes* to get treatment for his son, John pulls out his gun and proceeds to hijack the medical staff. He goes to these lengths only to try and save his son. As much as his actions seem drastic, I could fully understand his desperation and, in truth, I may have done the same thing for one of my kids.

John Q's willingness to do *whatever it takes* doesn't just stop at this point, as he is finally faced with the decision of giving his own heart to his son. In an act of total love and extreme commitment John Q allows doctors to take his heart and give it to his child. *Whatever it takes,* is not just a nice mantra for John Q – it is a radical act of sacrifice.

In *Chasing the Wind*, Michael Cassidy recounts how sacrificial love is imitated in the behaviour of animals, as well as in man. "Once there was a fire which swept across a farmyard. A mother hen and her chickens were right in its path. The mother hen saw quickly and clearly that she could not escape the flames, given the speed at which they were moving. So she nestled down over her chicks and the flames roared over her. Afterwards the scorched body of the mother her was found, but the little chicks beneath her were still alive. In her instinctive love she had given herself so that the little chicks might live. That is sacrificial love."[25]

Doing everything for your children can easily reach a point of becoming unhealthy. This may seem a strange thing to say, after all I have just mentioned, but let me explain. Modern schooling seems to demand more and more from our children. Coupled with this is a societal pressure for our kids to perform and be the best. As parents, we quickly buy into this mind set and before we realise it we are doing all we can to give our kids opportunities we never had. We rush around to extra-mural sports programmes, cultural performances, music lessons, falling into an exhausted heap on a Sunday, only to repeat the same thing the next week.

We are misguided if we think this is best for our kids. I have witnessed families stop worshipping regularly simply because they are too exhausted to travel again on a Sunday. Exhaustion is not a fabrication, but the lesson we teach our children can be misguided. They may just be learning:

"It's alright to do *whatever it takes* to achieve in sport or school, even if this means missing worship on a Sunday. God understands how busy we are!"

Of course God understands how busy we are, but I am not sure that God is simply going to allow our relationship with him to be damaged by our busy schedules.

Sometimes we need to let our children face difficulties in order to let them grow – as hard as that may be for us to witness. General Douglas MacArthur wrote this prayer for his son. He prayed:

"Build me a son, O Lord, who will be strong enough to know when he is weak, and brave enough to face himself when he is afraid. One who will be proud and unbending in honest defeat, and humble and gentle in victory.

"Build me a son whose wishes will not take the place of deeds - a son who will know Thee, who is the foundation stone of knowledge. Lead him, I pray, not in the path of ease & comfort, but under the stress & spur of difficulties & challenge.

"Here let him learn to stand up to the storm. Here let him learn compassion for those who fail. Build me a son whose heart will be clear, whose goal will be high, a son who will master himself before he seeks to master other men, one who will reach into the future, yet never forget the past.

"And after all these things are his, add, I pray, enough of a sense of humour so that he may always be serious but never take himself too seriously. Give him humility so that he may always remember the simplicity of true greatness, and an open mind of true wisdom, & the meekness of true strength.

"Then I, his father, will dare to whisper, 'I have not lived in vain.'

This is indeed a courageous prayer to utter. Hoping for the best for our children should not mean sparing them from difficulties or the realities of life. We could do more harm that way.

How are your family relationships at the moment? It is a reality that we may well be living in brokenness with people that share our homes, schools, office space and churches. Proximity is not an indication of healthy relationships. We can be living side by side with people, yet we may as well be living miles apart. Distance is not purely a metric measure – it can also be an indicator of the state of our relationships.

I firmly believe that doing *whatever it takes* ultimately hinges on a very important principle – that of choice. Choosing to be a bridge in your relationships with others may be the toughest decision you make today, but it could be the most rewarding. Do you really want to go to great lengths to make things right or are you just not bothered?

God is longing to restore what He made perfect in the Garden of Eden. God is willing to do *whatever it takes* to return us back to that former glory and to claim us as His children. This is evidenced in so many ways in the Scriptures, starting from helping the Israelites escape from Egypt, the rebuilding of the walls of Jerusalem and ultimately in sending Jesus into the world.

Can God help us to restore something that seems broken beyond repair? God is able to do the impossible – he can restore any broken relationship if we are willing to partner with him in this. *Whatever it takes* is God's mantra too!

- **Mark 10:27** - Jesus looked at them and said, 'With man this is **impossible**, but not with God; all things are possible with God.'

- **John 9:3-5** - Jesus said, "You're asking the wrong question. You're looking for someone to blame. There is no such cause-effect here. Look instead for what **God can** do." (Message)

TIME OF REFLECTION

1. Think about how things are at the moment with your spouse, children, parents, in-laws, siblings, colleagues. Is there a tension in any one of these relationships? Does it bother you that things are not 100% in these relationships? What are you prepared to do about it?

2. When you read the following quote from Dr. Arnold Mol, what thoughts impact you?

"No relationship can continue indefinitely, let alone grow, if it is not consciously worked on. Only people in fairy tales get married and 'live happily ever after'. In real life, we have to build our relationships with purposeful determination particularly since there are so many 'natural' forces which cause conflict and erode our relationship."

3. Read John 19:25-27 to see how highly Jesus valued his family. When you have finished reading this passage find Luke 15:20 and reflect on this verse.

97

____

____

____

4.   Think about your broader family for a moment. Why don't you offer a prayer of Thanksgiving for each one of them? Acknowledge what "imprint" they have left on your life and pray a blessing over them.

____

____

____

seven

FRIENDSHIP

TWO ARE BETTER THAN ONE

"Ninety percent of all people who fail in their life's vocation fail because they cannot get along with people."

- CARNEGIE INSTITUTE

"What a blessing ... to have a faithful friend."

- CHARLES SIMEON

The popular sitcom *Friends* debuted in September 1994 and during its ten year run won numerous awards. The catchy theme song '"I'll be there for you" summed up the overall message of each episode, with members of the cast offering companionship and help to their friends, despite their own struggles in life. The popularity of *Friends* was based on the genuineness of the friendships and the wonderful humour that accompanied each situation they found themselves in.

Paul Deitz tries to understand why this thirty minute sitcom became so hugely popular. He writes, "I tend to believe it all stems from our inborn instinct to want to have personal relationships with other people and to be able to know them as close friends. We love spending quality time with our friends. We all truly believe and practice the concept of this popular television series: "You can never have enough friends.""

This statement may be true, but what would you define as friendship? A newspaper publication once offered a prize for the best definition of a friend. There were thousands of answers sent into the paper, but some of the best responses included these insights:

"A friend is one who understands our silence."

"A friend is like a watch that beats true for all time and never runs down."

The editor eventually decided that the following definition deserved to win the prize:

"A friend is the one who comes in when the whole world has gone out." [26]

I like this definition. To have a friend is truly one of the greatest gifts we could enjoy. As I daily count my blessings, I am grateful that God has brought wonderful friends into my life. In each stage of my life, I have had the privilege of knowing many remarkable people. They all add value to my life, but there remain some friends who have been part of my life for nearly 30 years, and counting. It is these friends that will always be there for me, even if the rest of the world turns its back on me.

Perhaps you have friendships like this too? These are the kind of friendships that will span cities and continents; that will guide us through the seasons of kids, work changes, mid-life crisis and even times when crucial decisions have to be made. These friends will be friends for life. As Aristotle once said, "Friendship is a single soul dwelling in two bodies." I am truly blessed to know men and women like this.

Albert Durer and Franz Knigstein were two such friends. Albert Durer was a famous artist during the German Renaissance period. He was born in Nurnberg in 1471 and died there in 1528. You may have seen his famous wood cuttings of the horsemen of the Apocalypse. Durer is also famous for his *study of Praying Hands* which he completed in 1508. If you have never seen the painting I encourage you to look it up on the internet now – it may help you to appreciate the rest of the story.

What many people don't know is that the *Praying Hands* were modelled from those of his close friend, Franz Knigstein. As two young, poor, but aspiring artists they had made a pact. They drew 'straws' and the person who won would go to art school, while the other friend would work in order to support the other. When the one artist found fame, he would return and support the studies of his friend.

Albert drew the right straw and went off to art school. When he returned to Nurnberg a while later he found that Franz was gravely ill. His fingers were so disfigured through all the work that he had been doing, that he was never able to paint again. His fingers were so twisted and bent that holding a paint brush was impossible. Albert Durer was filled with much sadness for his friends' condition and humbled at the sacrifice he had made. One particular day, when he saw Franz praying, he became so moved by his friends' piety and devotion that he modelled his *Study of Praying Hands* on Franz' hands. The portrait became a witness to his friends' complete sacrifice and Durer never forgot this, as long as he lived. [27]

What an incredible story of friendship! For me, friendship goes much further than just inviting someone to be a friend on Facebook or Twitter. It is about being there for each other, no matter what it takes. A friend will stick it out with you until the very end. Gordon Macdonald sums up what it means to be a friend,

"A friend will stick it out with you until the very end."

"...special friends are committed to helping one another discover and maintain spiritual passion. Each member of a team of special friends rejoices when another succeeds. Each weeps when another fails. Special friends do not envy when someone wins; nor do they gloat at failure."[28]

Archbishop Emeritus, Desmond Tutu, has been in the press a lot lately. The storm began to brew when one of Desmond's friends, the Dali Lama, was refused a visitor's visa to attend his 80th birthday celebrations a few years ago. Obvious political connections were cited as the reason for this, but whatever the ultimate reasons were, Desmond Tutu was not happy. He has always been an outspoken person, especially when it comes to issues of justice and equality. However, his strong reaction caused the National Government to do some serious thinking when he openly admitted he was praying for the downfall of the ANC government.

Let's put our political bias aside for a moment and think about this statement – any public person willing to stand up and say these things either has to be crazy or profoundly prophetic. Tutu was not afraid of the consequences and was willing to stand by his convictions. If we had been living in a different era (which was actually not too long ago) he would have been arrested for his comments. *Whatever it takes* means exactly that – *whatever it takes* to speak out for truth, we must be prepared to do so. A friend is always willing to speak out in our defence, no matter the cost.

At the moment I am re-reading *Band of Brothers*, by Stephen Ambrose. It tells the story of Easy Company, who trained together and then were involved in the D-Day invasion of 1944. There are so many remarkable stories that come out of their war experiences, but the theme of friendship stands out for me. These men were thrown together by a situation that was out of their control, and yet the horrors of war forged friendships that would last a lifetime. As Ambrose puts it, *"within Easy Company they had made the best friends they had ever had, or would ever have. They were prepared to die for each other."* [29]

So it seems that genuine friendship involves a willingness to put aside our own desires and to be ready to sacrifice for someone else. The Bible speaks of friendship in numerous places, but of course we need not look any further than Jesus' example of friendship. He was willing to do *whatever it takes* for his friends and ultimately for us. These are the words of Jesus recorded in John's gospel:

"No greater love has a man than this, that he is willing to lay down his life for his friends."[30]

I think that Jesus took great delight in referring to the disciples as his friends and I am sure that their hearts swelled with pride when he did just that. Who wouldn't want to be called a friend of Jesus? A few verses later on in John chapter 15, we read another powerful statement from Jesus:

"I no longer call you servants, because a servant does not know his master's business. Instead, I have called you friends."[31]

Jesus was the kind of friend who not only spoke of love and sacrifice, but who showed his friends that he really meant it. His words were never hollow or empty – Jesus followed through with every one of his promises.

There are also other examples of biblical characters who displayed great friendship. David and Jonathan's friendship survived the turbulence of King Saul's anger, which obviously placed Jonathan in a number of awkward situations. When your father hates your best friend, it can be spell the end of that friendship, but this was not the case with these two great friends.

Jonathan said to David, "Go in peace, for we have sworn friendship with each other in the name of the LORD, saying, 'The LORD is witness between you and me, and between your descendants and my descendants forever.'" Then David left, and Jonathan went back to the town.[32]

So let me get to my point.

How are your friendships at the moment?

Are they doing okay or are you perhaps dealing with a broken friendship in your life? Has an issue with a close friend gotten out of hand and now you find yourself experiencing the painful fallout of this friendship? If any one of these applies to you, then ask yourself this hard question:

Am I willing to do whatever it takes to restore this friendship?

Please don't misunderstand me. I am not naively assuming that you don't have a right to be angry or hurt by some action from these particular friends. What I am suggesting is take a closer look at what Jesus taught in the Bible on the topic of forgiveness and friendship. Is it possible that God could be calling you to go the extra mile in order to restore this friendship? Even David experienced brokenness in his some of his friendships. These are his words,

> "Even my close friend, whom I trusted, he who shared my bread, has lifted up his heel against me. . . If an enemy were insulting me, I could endure it; if a foe were raising himself against me, I could hide from him. But it is you, a man like myself, my companion, my close friend, with whom I once enjoyed sweet fellowship as we walked with the throng at the house of God."[33]

Before you read any further please pause and do a little soul-searching. Ask the Holy Spirit to call to mind your friends and to prompt you to some action. Life is far too short to bear any grudges – friendships are worth fighting for.

Friends also play a crucial role in supporting us through difficult times. They are there to hold us up when life threatens to drag us down. This seems to be Solomon's experience as he makes this comment:

"Two are better than one,
  because they have a good return for their labour:
  If either of them falls down,
  one can help the other up.
  But pity anyone who falls
  and has no one to help them up."[34]

I am not sure if you can remember the story of Moses and his two friends, Aaron and Hur? It is told in Exodus 17:8-13:

The Amalekites came and attacked the Israelites at Rephidim. Moses said to Joshua, "Choose some of our men and go out to fight the Amalekites. Tomorrow I will stand on top of the hill with the staff of God in my hands."

So Joshua fought the Amalekites as Moses had ordered, and Moses, Aaron and Hur went to the top of the hill. As long as Moses held up his hands, the Israelites were winning, but whenever he lowered his hands, the Amalekites were winning. When Moses' hands grew tired, they took a stone and put it under him and he sat on it. Aaron and Hur held his hands up—one on one side, one on the other— so that his hands remained steady till sunset. So Joshua overcame the Amalekite army with the sword.

There is a powerful lesson in this story - friends can help each other accomplish more than we can achieve on our own. We all need people to lean on and to support us in our times of need. Do you have such people in your life at the moment?

What are you doing to nurture those relationships?

Recently we watched the movie, *The Kings Speech*. It is a moving account of how two men (King George VI and Lionel Logue) help each other overcome the huge obstacles that present themselves before them. Both men display a *whatever it takes* attitude, although in totally different ways. After the death of his father King George V and the abdication of his brother (King Edward VIII), Bertie is suddenly crowned King George VI of England. However, Bertie has suffered from a speech impediment that has left him withdrawn and severely lacking in confidence. Needless to say this presents a massive stumbling block to the King as public speaking is not optional for him.

So with England on the brink of war and in desperate need of a leader, Bertie's wife, Elizabeth, arranges for him to visit a speech therapist, Lionel Logue. Against all odds, these two men forge a unique friendship that transcends class and social standing. Lionel Logue helps the King to overcome his stammer and to deliver a radio-address that inspires the nation.

For me, *The King's Speech* is a remarkable story of friendship and hope. It reminds me of the many times I have had to lean on the support of a trusted friend. True friends help us confront our worst fears and then to overcome these obstacles with strength and courage.

In his book *Encouragement: Oxygen for the Soul*, Derick Bingham tells a lovely story of his Scottish friend William McClachlan. He uses the story to show how we need people to help us live our lives well. We need friends who can immediately tell what we need and who are willing to show us the way.

As a child, William often used to fly his kite. One particular day he was out in the field trying to get his kite to lift into the air. It kept lifting off the ground, but then flying erratically and falling to the ground. A passer-by noticed what was happening and approached William saying, "What you need is a divot to your draigon, sonny" (sic)

"A what?" asked William.

"A divot to your draigon!" He replied.

As he said this, the man leaned down and picked up a small clod of earth and grass and proceed to tie it to the kite string. When William flew the kite again it soared perfectly. The divot gave the kite weight and balance.[35]

I know that I often need to regain my balance, so that I can fly with Christ. There are too many days where we struggle along in our faith, starting and then falling to the ground. We need to search for the right kind of 'divot' to keep us rooted in Christ and perfectly balanced. For me, this is when I need to turn to my trusted friends. They are the ones who can be honest with me, especially when I feel out of balance. If they don't keep me accountable then I know that I will be 'flying' erratically and it could spell disaster for my family and community.

Another one of the crucial ingredients in a friendship is the ability to offer and receive thanks. We should never engage in friendships only because we want some form of gratification, but we should be willing to show our gratitude to those who have shown themselves to be loyal and influential in our lives. The following story reveals something of what I am trying to convey.

In the midst of the Great Depression, Professor William Stidger of the School of theology in Boston, was challenged to think of the blessings he had received in his life. He remembered his old kindergarten teacher, who had greatly impacted his life, but whom he had never taken the time to thank. His teacher had believed in him and had become a friend to him. So he immediately sat down and wrote a letter to her. A few days later, he received the following reply, written in an aged scrawl:

> *Dear Willie,*
>
> *I cannot tell you how much your note meant to me. I am in my eighties, living alone in a small room, cooking my own meals, lonely and like the last leaf in Autumn, lingering behind. You will be interested to know that I taught school for fifty years and yours is the first note of appreciation I ever received. It came on a blue-cold morning and it cheered me as nothing has in many years.*

Today may just be the day that we need to get in touch with some old friends. There may be some of our friends who need a message of encouragement right now. Please don't let this moment pass you by – drop them a line, send them a text message or perhaps even send them an email. It could just end up being the very thing that makes their day.

John Maxwell commented that when it comes to friendships, "either we are pulling together or we are pulling apart." So what do we do when we sense that our friendships are pulling apart? The reality is that most of us have a sorry tale of a broken friendship. This may have been at their doing or even ours – but the memory of that incident may jar in our minds from time to time. If our friendships are worth keeping, then when they begin to show signs of strain then it is worth trying to save them and to speak through the relevant issues.

There are a few times in my life where I have either had to have honest 'heart to heart' conversations with some friends and they, in turn, have also had the chance to do the same for me. I am not a confrontational person by nature, but when something as valuable as friendship is on the line, then I am willing to go the extra mile. I can honestly say that these friendships are actually the ones that have lasted the longest. Honesty, spoken in love, should never kill a friendship.

When a friendship is valued then we should be willing to do all we can to save it and to nurture it. Friends should love at all times and be willing to go through thick and thin with us. True friends are not people who turn around and desert you when times are tough.

As Jeremy Taylor once remarked, "by friendship you mean the greatest love, the greatest usefulness, the most open communication, the noblest sufferings, the severest truth, the heartiest counsel, and the greatest union of minds of which brave men and women are capable." What a wonderful way of describing our friendships.

We have often heard the saying, "a dog is a man's best friend!" This is certainly true in many instances and I think it is because our dogs are so forgiving of our bad behaviour. I know that our black Labrador Bella certainly treats me as her best friend, despite the many times I have had to chastise her. One moment we can be having words with her, usually for chewing our flowerpots or the kids' toys, but the next second she will be rolling over, waiting for us to tickle her belly. Dogs certainly know how to forgive easily!

I stumbled across the remarkable story of a dog named Hachikō and seeing as we are on the topic of friendship and dogs, I thought it would be worth sharing. We could all learn a lot from this furry friend.
In the beginning of 1924, Professor Ueno was working in the agricultural department at the University of Tokyo. He was looking for a trusted

companion and so Professor Ueno found a golden brown Akita, and took him as his pet. He named his new dog, Hachikō, and the two were inseparable.

Professor Ueno used to catch the train to work every day and Hachikō would greet him at the end of his work day at the nearby Shibuya Station. The pair continued this daily routine until one day in May 1925, when Professor Ueno never returned. It was only discovered later that the professor had suffered a cerebral haemorrhage and subsequently died, thus never returning to the train station where Hachikō was waiting.

Of course no one was able to communicate this to his loyal dog and so each day for the next nine years Hachikō ran to the train station to wait for Professor Ueno. Hachiko would appear precisely at the same time when the train was due to arrive at the station. If you visit the Shibuya Station today you will find a statue of this incredible dog standing proudly outside the entrance of the station – waiting for his best friend.

As Benjamin Franklin once remarked, "be slow in choosing a friend and slower in changing." Friendship is indeed a remarkable gift and we should be willing to do *whatever it takes* to maintain these treasures.

As we conclude this chapter, I want to share this challenging poem on friendship, written by Henson Towne. It is entitled, *Around the Corner*.

Around the corner I have a friend,
In this great city that has no end.
Yet days go by and weeks rush on,
And before I know it a year is gone,
And I never see my old friend's face;

For life is a swift and terrible race.

He knows I like him just as well
As in the days when I rang his bell
And he rang mine. We were younger then -
And now we are busy, tired men -
Tired with playing a foolish game;
Tired with trying to make a name.

"Tomorrow," I say, "I will call on Jim,
Just to show that I'm thinking of him."
But tomorrow comes - and tomorrow goes;
And the distance between us grows and grows.
Around the corner - yet miles away...

"Here's a telegram, sir."
"Jim died today."
And that's what we get - and deserve in the end -
Around the corner, a vanished friend. [36]

May God bless you in your friendships and may you do *whatever it takes* to keep and restore important friendships in your life.

TIME OF REFLECTION

1.	What key thought on Friendship will you take away from this chapter?

2.	Reflecting on the story of the kite, earlier in this chapter, who is the person who helps to keep you 'flying' correctly? Have you taken the time to thank them for the role they play in your life?

3.	Are there some friendships in your life that need to be repaired? Are they worth fighting for?

4.   How do the words of the following song make you feel?

"What a friend we have in Jesus,
All our sins and griefs to bear.
Oh what privilege to carry,
Everything to God in prayer."

5.   Do you have a close friendship with Jesus at the moment? Why or why not?

eight

FAITH

PERSEVERING UNTIL THE END

"Catch on fire for God and people will come for miles to see you burn."

- JOHN WESLEY

"Jesus tells us to set our hearts on the kingdom. Setting our hearts on something involves not only our serious aspiration but also strong determination."

- HENRI NOUWEN

Romanian Pastor, Richard Wurmbrand, was imprisoned for 14 years for his faith in Jesus Christ. During this time he was physically and psychologically tortured – all in an attempt to make him renounce his faith. It was only his incredibly strong relationship with Jesus that kept him sane during these horrendous years. He was prepared to stand up for Jesus, no matter what his captors did to him.

He remembers that no prisoners were allowed to have pens, pencils or paper, yet he managed to still write. He smeared soap on the soles of a shoe and wrote on it with a piece of wood. In this way he managed to write 350 Romanian poems, which he committed to memory, and transcribed after his release from prison. [37]

So if we thought that following Jesus was going to be easy, we need to think again! If you were ever told that being a Christ-follower was going to be simple and filled with applause and acclaim, well someone lied to you! Following Jesus will be the hardest thing you ever do in your life. It has certainly been like that for me. Of course I have experienced many days of celebration, but there have been equally many days of struggle. If we want to 'succeed' in being a Christ-follower we need to be willing to embrace the *whatever it takes* spirit. We will need to hang on tight, grit our teeth and steel ourselves for battle.

Can we imagine what would have happened if Jesus had not had the will to go to the cross? We remember his agonising in the Garden of Gethsemane – he knew what lay in store for him – yet he somehow managed to pray, "Not my will, but yours be done!" At a glance, it seems to me, that Jesus 'willed' something else – he wanted to love people, but he was not looking forward to the painful death on a cross. His human will wrestled with what he knew his Father wanted. In the end, Jesus did whatever was necessary to win salvation for all of us. His sacrifice impacted every human being, whether we accept his love and mercy or not.

This really humbles me. I think about other times in my life, where I have not wanted to do something, just because I didn't feel up to it or have the will to go through with it. And so, in order to please myself, I never bothered finding a way to get the task done. Who did I rob, by choosing the selfish route?

There is a powerful passage in the New Testament that is well worth reflecting on. It is the encounter that takes place between Jesus and the rich young ruler (Matthew 19:16-26). I just want to highlight a few key points about this interaction. First, we note that the young man is feeling unfulfilled in his current experience of religion. He says clearly to Jesus, "All of these (laws) I have kept....but what do I still lack?" (Matthew 19:20)

There was obviously something missing in his life and in his relationship with God. He wanted to do *whatever it takes* to make things better, even asking Jesus, "Teacher, what good thing must I do to get eternal life?" Perhaps in his mind he thought he was ready to do *whatever it takes*, but in the end, we see that he wasn't really. When Jesus presented him with the answer to his crisis, he wasn't prepared to follow through with this.

If we take a quick glance at the commandments the young man was following, all of them were in respect to his relationships with other people: "Do not murder. Do not commit adultery. Do not steal. Do not give false testimony. Honour your father and mother. Love your neighbour as yourself" (Matthew 19:18-19).

By all appearances, this rich young man was a nice guy. Perhaps the kind of guy many mothers would want their daughters to meet and marry! However, when Jesus challenges him on a deeper level, he pinpoints the rich young man's greatest obstacle – his love of wealth. If this young man wanted to genuinely do *whatever it takes*, he would have seen that Jesus' word to him – 'sell all you have and give to the poor' was a direct reference to the First Commandment (Exodus 20:3).

So, this was his stumbling block. The doctor had prescribed the medicine, but he was not prepared to take it. He walked away disappointed and empty, because deep inside he knew he still longed for something more, but he wasn't prepared to do *whatever it takes*.

Many years after this story, St Augustine penned a thought, which encapsulates the emotions of this young man: "Our hearts are restless until they find their rest in you O' Lord." This was true in my experience. I had tried a number of different things in life, before I eventually turned to Jesus. Although the other goals and achievements initially offered me some sense of purpose, they still left me feeling empty. It was only when I was willing to surrender my life into the hands of God, that I discovered a renewed direction and fulfilment.

Bilquis Sheikh's story is another truly remarkable account of someone willing to lay down their life for Jesus. Her story is told in the wonderful book *"I dared to call him Father."* Growing up as a Muslim woman, Bilquis had a life changing encounter with Jesus Christ and she then converted to Christianity. It is no small matter to say the words, "I am a Christian," when the rest of your community strongly opposes Christianity. So, when Bilquis' family found out about her conversion, they called a family meeting and gave her an ultimatum:

"Remember, Bilquis, if you get into trouble, none of your friends or family can stand by you. The ones who care most will have to turn their backs on you."

This is exactly what she had to endure, yet Bilquis was willing to go through the trauma of family rejection because she understood how much Jesus loved her. She had dared to call him Father and now God had changed her life. It is true that choosing to follow Jesus can never be a choice for comfort.

This simple gravestone tells the remarkable story of Bilquis' life:

Born 12-12-12

Died 9-4-97

Loving the Lord [38]

We will also find evidence of people willing to go to great lengths for their faith, in the Biblical book of Daniel. This prophetic book is filled with accounts of how Daniel and his friends were willing to do anything to honour God.

Firstly, we see how Daniel refused to eat food from the King's table. It is not an easy thing to turn down good food from a powerful King, especially when Nebuchadnezzar had the authority to order your head to be chopped off.

The second incident, which reveals Daniel's *whatever it takes* mind-set, is when he interprets the Kings dream. Daniel walks into the palace of a non-believer and says to him: "No wise man, enchanter, magician or diviner can explain to the king the mystery he has asked about, but there is a God in heaven who reveals mysteries" (Daniel 2:27-28).

Daniel's bravery is well timed of course, as the king is desperate to understand his dream, but we shouldn't minimise the huge amount of courage it took from this young man.

Thirdly, we see how his three friends stood up to King Nebuchadnezzar. Shadrach, Meshach and Abednego replied to the king,

> *"O Nebuchadnezzar, we do not need to defend ourselves before you in this matter. If we are thrown into the blazing furnace, the God we serve is able to save us from it, and he will rescue us from your hand, O King. But even if he does not, we want you to know, O King, that we will not serve your gods or worship the image of gold you have set up" (Daniel 3: 16-18).*

Well, that is a lesson in how to win friends and influence people! The King was so angry he ordered the furnace made 7 times hotter and threw all three of them into the fire. It was only some time later that he realised the men had not been burnt to cinders and so he called them out of the fire. Oh, how I would have wanted to be a fly on the King's turban then. He was gobsmacked and declared, "No other god can save in this way!" (Daniel 3:29) That has to be the understatement of history!

Author Gordon Macdonald sums it up nicely when he writes, "It is a dangerous thing – a very dangerous thing – to have a skimpy impression of the Almighty God. But that is the state of millions upon millions of people whose perspective of the Creator and his purposes is so puny that He has become virtually the last thing they respect or fear." [39]

Has God called you to something that you are scared to respond to? What is making you the most fearful about this calling? Are you prepared to do *whatever it takes* in response to this?

One of my fellow Ministers, Rev. Nelson Chacate, was born in Mozambique. When he arrived in South Africa to begin his theological training, he was not able to speak English and isiZulu, although he could speak Portuguese and Ronga fluently. Nelson knew that the Lord had called him to ministry and he has been willing to do *whatever it takes* to improve and learn the local languages. Nelson can now speak 5 languages and he preaches powerfully and coherently to our communities in English and isiZulu.

But, this is only half of his story. Nelson's testimony is deeply moving. He received his calling into the ministry whilst he was still in Mozambique, but he had not always been in the church. His parents were killed by Renamo soldiers during the war and he grew up hating other people. He also had to endure the pain of losing his brother in mysterious circumstances in 2010. Despite all of the trauma Nelson has encountered, God has worked an incredible healing in his life and he is now a wonderful minister of the Gospel. Perhaps these words of the Apostle Paul's could echo Nelson's deepest desire:
"I consider my life worth nothing to me, if only I may finish the race and complete the task the Lord Jesus has given me – the task of testifying to the gospel of God's grace."(Acts 20:24)

If ever there is an example of someone who was willing to do *whatever it takes* to win people for Jesus Christ, it has to be the apostle Paul. The verse below gives us such a clear insight into how he tried to minister to everyone.

"I have become a servant of everyone so that I can bring them to Christ." -
1 Corinthians 9:19-23

Some people refer to this as a Chameleon faith – and in a positive sense, Paul was a Chameleon. He tried to blend into the environment of every community, so that he could have a platform to preach the good news. This is obviously a dangerous tactic for the spiritually immature person, but Paul had been through enough hardship in his religious life, to recognise danger when he saw it. His *whatever it takes* attitude made him one of the most effective missionaries ever.

Of course, Paul's willingness to morph into a different person, depending on the circumstances, was not new. God had already played that card in the form of Jesus Christ. The very word, 'Incarnation', speaks of the Word becoming flesh and dwelling amongst us. John does a great job of highlighting this mystery in the first chapter of the Gospel. God knew that the only way to get a message through to humanity was to become human. Jesus took on our nature and form, in order to effectively give us the message of his Father's unconditional love.

The Carthusian Order of the middle Ages had a motto *'Mundus Mihi Crucifixus Est'* – which translates as follows:
"The world is my Crucifix!"

If ever there was a motto that speaks of the *whatever it takes* spirit, it is this one! Doing *whatever it takes* to answer the calling from God will always come at a great cost.

I am deeply fascinated by the story behind the much loved hymn, *I have decided to Follow Jesus*. It has been attributed to a few writers, but one of them is S. Sundar Singh. The story behind the song is covered in the book 'Why God Why?' (Dr. P.P. Job) and is set in the North-East region of India.[40] The region was known as Assam and comprised hundreds of tribes. The tribal communities were quite primitive and aggressive by nature.

A number of the tribes were also called head-hunters. This stemmed from a social custom which required the men of the community to collect as many human heads as possible. A man's strength and ability to protect his family was assessed by the number of heads he managed to collect - sounds a bit too gruesome for me. Young men of marriageable age would try and collect as many heads as possible and hang them on the walls of their house. The more heads a man had, the more eligible he was considered to be.

A group of Welsh missionaries came into this part of India, spreading the message of love, peace and hope of Jesus Christ. They were not welcomed with open arms and faced many difficulties. One of the missionarys succeeded in converting a local family – a husband, his wife, and their two children. This man's faith proved contagious and many villagers began to accept Christianity. Angry, the village chief summoned all the villagers. He then called the family who had first converted to renounce their faith in public or face execution. He threatened that the two children would be killed first.

According to the story, the father was moved by the Spirit and instantly composed the words to a song. He sang:

I have decided to follow Jesus
I have decided to follow Jesus

I have decided to follow Jesus
No turning back, no turning back.

Enraged at the refusal of the man, the chief ordered his archers to arrow down the two children. As both boys lay twitching on the floor, the chief asked, "Will you deny your faith? You have lost both your children. You will lose your wife too." But the man sang these words in reply:

Though None Go With Me, Still I Will Follow
Though None Go With Me, Still I Will Follow
Though None Go With Me, Still I Will Follow
No Turning Back, No Turning Back.

The chief was beside himself with fury and ordered his wife to be shot. She too joined her two children in death. Now the chief asked for the last time, "I will give you one more opportunity to deny your faith and live. You have no one else to live for, but you can live yourself!"
In the face of death the man sang the final memorable lines:

The World Behind Me, The Cross Before Me
The World Behind Me, The Cross Before Me
The World Behind Me, The Cross Before Me
No Turning Back, No Turning Back.

He was shot dead like the rest of his family. If the story ended there, it would just be depressing, but thankfully a miracle took place. The chief who had ordered the killings was moved by the faith of the man and his family. He wondered, "Why should this man, his wife and two children die for a Man who lived in a far-away land on another continent some 2,000 years ago? There must be some supernatural power behind the family, and I too want that supernatural power." In a spontaneous confession of faith, the chief declared, "I too belong to Jesus Christ!" When the crowd heard this from the mouth of their chief, the whole village accepted Christ as their Lord and Saviour. This is the power of God in demonstration. As John Flavel once remarked, "true Christianity is all-out commitment to Jesus Christ."

In our modern churches we don't think of persecution as being 'blessed.' We rather shy away from as much pain as possible and to contemplate suffering is to admit defeat. Yet, for thousands of years our spiritual ancestors encountered persecution and suffering on a daily basis. They counted it a privilege to suffer for the name of Christ. In fact, they thought they had done something wrong when they weren't being abused, arrested and condemned.

Some of the early church leaders, such as Justin Martyr, sought the truth in all kinds of other places, before he accepted Christ. Once he had understood that Jesus was his Saviour Justin set out to explain the Gospel to the world. He is known as an Apologist, as he had the ability to defend and explain the Christian faith to unbelievers. He used his gift of writing and intellect to offer principles and guidance to the church. Living in Rome in the middle of the 2nd century was not easy for Christians. As a Christian teacher and philosopher, Justin faced opposition and ridicule. He so angered the Romans that he was eventually beheaded for his faith. That is why we know him as Justin Martyr. He is but one example of hundreds of Christians willing to do *whatever it takes* to worship Jesus and to speak for truth.

Luke records how Jesus was walking along a road, when a man came up to Jesus and said, "I will follow you wherever you go." (Luke 9:57) Knowing what was in the man's heart Jesus decided to push him a little further – are you really willing to do *whatever it takes* my friend? In a way, Jesus was asking him to count the cost fully before he decided to follow him, so he says, "foxes have holes and birds of the air have nests, but the Son of Man has no place to lay his head." (v.58)

Why does Jesus seem so harsh on this guy? Perhaps, Jesus knew that this man valued comfort more than sacrifice. We should never follow Jesus under the false pretence that this is an easy choice. If we pitched the Gospel higher, we may not have as many people come forward to say yes, but those that would come forward would be fully committed to Jesus.

A missionary society wrote to David Livingstone and asked, "Have you found a good road to where you are? If so, we want to know how to send other men to join you." Livingstone wrote back, "If you have men who will come only if they know there is a good road, I don't want them. I want men who will come if there is no road at all." [41]

There was another person walking with the disciples, who presumably overheard Jesus' comment, so when Jesus invited this man to follow him, the second man replied, "Lord, first let me go and bury my father." (v.59)

Jesus reply often seems harsh to us, but he says, "Let the dead bury their own dead, but you go and proclaim the kingdom of God." We don't know if the man's father was already dead, which seems unlikely, as he would have already been with his family. Perhaps his father was ill and was not expected to live long; we don't know for sure. There is even a possibility that the man's father was in good health and a long way from death – it would have been his responsibility as a son to take care of the burial plans and so on – so he was delaying his decision to follow Jesus until some future date.

Whatever the situation, Jesus was clearly saying that we can't delay in following him. Perhaps it could be like us saying, "I will follow Jesus when my kids have grown up or less demanding!" "I will follow Jesus when I have retired!" I will follow Jesus when I am not so committed elsewhere!"

There will always be some inconvenience to keep us from following Jesus, but we need to get to a point of saying, "I will follow Christ, *whatever it takes!*"

Jesus is making the point that the crucial point in that man's life is *NOW* – not later. The Spirit was stirring in his heart right there and then – if he waited longer he may not get another chance to follow Jesus. A few years ago I wrote a little book entitled *NOW* - it was written after the tragic death of a close friend. Through the tragedy of his death I found myself consumed by the desire never to put something off until later, if it could be done today. This is especially relevant to the people that we love and our valued friendships.

There was a third man who also claimed to be willing to follow Jesus, but he first wanted to go back and say good bye to his family. That seems like a reasonable request to me, but Jesus turns to him and says: "No one who puts his hand to the plough and looks back is fit for service in the kingdom of God" (Luke 9:57-62).

If you picture a person ploughing a field, you will know that if you keep looking back, you will not plough a straight line – you will be all over the place. It is the same as running in a race – if you keep looking around at your opponents you will not come first (I keep telling the kids this!) – If our hearts are always looking back to the past, we will never see what God has in store for us in the future. Are you willing to let go of the past and look to the future?

Again, Jesus makes the point that we can't follow him at our convenience and according to our agenda. Radical obedience means we have to be prepared to embrace the cross, as well as the reward of the crown.

While we were travelling in Galloway, in Southern Scotland, during the June of 2011, we loved encountering the numerous historical sites along this ancient shoreline. I love places that are steeped in history. I find it mysterious, marvellous and moving! During this week we learnt about the Covenanters – a group of Christians who had broken away from the institutional Roman Catholic Church. They started off as a group of passionate believers, who were truly prepared to do *whatever it takes* to worship Christ in the way they felt free to do. Despite their best intentions, this decision obviously didn't go down too well with the religion of the day and the Covenanters were forced into many tragic situations.

One account records how two women, Margaret Wilson and Margaret McLachlan, were captured in the May of 1658. They were threatened with death, unless they recanted their heretical new faith and turned back to the true Catholic Church. These loyal mothers refused and so, as punishment, they were tied to stakes out in the Solway Firth, at low tide. They would have to endure the most prolonged of deaths, as they watched the tide slowly come in, covering at first their ankles, knees, waists, shoulders and finally covering their mouths, drowning them. That's a long time to consider whether you have made the right decision or not! *Whatever it takes* is not a decision on a whim, or after a night on the town. It is a calculated, life changing comprehension that we can't carry on in one direction any longer – we can do nothing more, but consciously move in another direction.

In his best seller, *The Search for Significance*, Robert McGee, reminds us that following Jesus does not depend on supernatural feelings all the time. If we rely on these feelings to dictate our relationship with God, then we find ourselves waiting for 'feelings' to motivate us. He says, "Some of us won't get up in the morning until the Lord 'tells us to.' We may not want to share Christ with others until we feel that God is prompting us. What we may be forgetting is that Christianity is primarily faith in action. Our emotions are not the most reliable source of motivation. Yes, the Holy Spirit does sometimes prompt us through impressions, but he has already given us the vast majority of what He wants us to do through the Scriptures. Rather than waiting for a 'holy zap' to get us going, we need to believe the truth of God's Word and take action for his glory."[42]

I have found these words to be poignantly true in my own life. There are days when I wake up and I honestly don't feel like doing my devotions. Sometimes I don't feel spiritual enough to preach and so I don't feel like going to minister at Church. However, I know that I need to give God time and space to speak to me, so I submit myself to the discipline of reading his Word. Even if I am not blown away by the reading for the day, I firmly believe that God is filling me with 'good things.' I also know that if I don't pitch up at the Church services, that someone else is going to be running around trying to find a sermon to preach – not only is that unfair, but I don't think my leaders would thank me for that. Doing *whatever it takes* to follow Jesus can never rely on my feelings as my primary motivating factor. Neither can it be yours.

"Doing whatever it takes to answer the calling from God will always come at a great cost."

Professor of Biblical Studies, John Dominic Crossan, invites us to imagine 3 different responses to Jesus. These responses are from people who have all heard and seen the same words and deeds of Jesus Christ:

He's dangerous, let's oppose him.

He's a criminal, let's execute him.

He's divine, let's follow him.

Jesus encountered all three of these responses in his lifetime. To the religious leaders of his day, the Scribes, Pharisees and Chief Priests, Jesus was dangerous. They declared him a blasphemer and a drunkard, a friend of sinners and a trouble causer. They did whatever they could to oppose him.

To the Roman authorities Jesus seemed a nuisance. Herod was threatened by this new King, Pilate was troubled by his claims of truth and the soldiers deemed him a mad-man and a criminal. They made a public spectacle of him and nailed him to a cross. They succeeded in doing whatever it took to silence the new King of the Jews.

To his friends and disciples Jesus was Divine. They knew that he spoke with authority and the miracles he performed were more than just magic – Jesus had the power to change lives and to bring hope. He preached about love and forgiveness. More than that, Jesus actually practised what he preached. They gave up everything to follow him, for nothing was going to stop them from walking in the ways of Christ. Who is Jesus to you and me? He may be dangerous to our status quo. Some of his claims may seem ludicrous to us. His love certainly seems revolutionary. But, if I see and believe that Jesus is the Son of God, then I have to be willing to do whatever it takes to follow him. His invitation is still out there – anyone can respond!

"If anyone would come after me, he must deny himself and take up his cross and follow me. For whoever wants to save his life will lose it, but whoever loses his life for me will save it." – Luke 9:23-24

TIME OF REFLECTION

As we move onto the next chapter, it is appropriate for us to pause for a minute. I encourage you to reflect on your personal faith journey and then to ask yourself these questions:

1. How are things going on your faith journey at the moment? Be honest and rate your relationship with Jesus Christ (out of 10).

2. Are you finding that your faith is just plodding along and even a little cold? Could the words from Revelation 3:14-22 be for you today?

3. If you answered 'yes' to the previous question, is it not time then to challenge yourself to go a little deeper with Christ? How will you do that?

4. Is there a spiritual mentor that you can make an appointment to see? It is helpful to speak through our faith struggles/victories with another Christ-follower. Why don't you do this today?

5. Contemplating all that Christ did for you, are you willing to do *whatever it takes* for Jesus?

nine

FELLOWSHIP

SURVIVING PRICKLY ISSUES IN THE CHURCH

"It requires less character to discover the faults of others than it does to tolerate them."

- J. PETIT-SENN

"But if we walk in the light, as he is in the light, we have fellowship with one another."

1 JOHN 1:7

German Philosopher, Schopenhauer once remarked that Christians are like a pack of porcupines on a freezing cold night. The freezing weather conditions force the porcupines together for warmth, but as they get closer to each other their quills begin to jab and wound each other. So they move away from each other, only to repeat the process over and over again.

I think this brilliantly describes the dilemma of Christian fellowship. True community is difficult – just when you feel it is all going well, then suddenly something bursts the bubble and people feel wounded. Over the years of ministry in various churches I have discovered that relationships within a community of faith are complex. In the very place where we should be showing love and care for each another, we often discover that this is not the case.

I am not sure if you have ever experienced divisive issues in your church at all? If you haven't as yet, then I urge you to pray for strength now, because those issues will come! Believe me there is no such thing as a perfect church community. If you think there is, then perhaps you should leave before you discover that 'all' people are flawed.

I strongly feel that when divisive issues arise in the midst of the body of Christ, we need to do all we can to resolve these issues. Sometimes, these issues may need time and healing in order to bring resolution, but this doesn't mean we must back off from trying to resolve them. David Watson states that "more than ever the Church needs to recapture the priority of community in Christian discipleship." I couldn't agree with him more.

We notice that the Greek word for fellowship *koinonia* means 'common' or 'shared.' If we use these words as a starting point, we note that fellowship implies a common participation in something – usually this revolves around our times of worship. Our worship experience is focused on the person of Jesus Christ – this is the 'common' platform from which we then begin to share in our fellowship. In essence, give and take becomes key in our fellowship, as we seek to live out Christ's example, within the body of Christ.

This may be a helpful definition to use as a starting point, but as you may have already discovered, it is never as simple as that. People are people and sooner or later, someone usually makes the goal of 'common' and 'shared' hard to live out.

Author and pastor, James Packer, suggests that Christian fellowship is essentially two-dimensional – horizontal and vertical. We must come to know the reality of fellowship with God (vertical) before we can truly know the reality of fellowship with each other (horizontal). It is our relationship with God that ultimately unites us in common, as God's people (1 John 1:3). James Packer goes so far as to suggest that "the person who is not in fellowship with the Father and the Son is no Christian at all, and so cannot share with Christians the realities of their fellowship." [43]

I would like to put forward two reasons why I feel we need to strive to maintain fellowship in the Christian community. It is for these reasons that we should do *whatever it takes* to facilitate unity in the body of Christ.

1.   *The Witness of the Church*

The first reason is that I believe the integrity of the Church witness is at stake. There was a time when Jesus spoke strongly to his disciples, "a new command I give you; Love one another. As I have loved you, so you must love one another. By this all people will know that you are my disciples, if you love one another" (John 13:35).

Did you notice what he was saying? Jesus is being direct about one important thing – the world will see how much we love him, by the way we love one another. In other words, our witness is at stake in all of this. If we fail to recognise this, then our divisions in the body of Christ do damage all around – within and without the community of faith.

When a Church splits over silly issues, there is much pain and the church becomes the centre of negative publicity. I remember reading a story about how a small Baptist church in rural America went through a Church split and they became the laughing stock of their community. The reason they split was over a humble clothes hook – can you believe that – a silly clothes hook caused a church community to be divided?

This church was home to two influential leaders and they took delight in disagreeing with each other the whole time. One evening their leaders' meeting contained an item on the agenda that seemed harmless enough – it was around the issue of placing a clothes hook in the vestry so that the minister would have a place to hang his coat during the service. Needless to say these two men disagreed on the appropriate place for the clothes hook and they ended up polarising the rest of the leadership. In the end, this simple matter caused a massive ripple effect in the community and the church eventually split. What kind of witness was this?

Legend has it that when the French and British were fighting in Canada in the 1750s, Admiral Phipps, commander of the British fleet, was told to anchor outside Quebec. He was instructed to wait for the British land forces to arrive, and then to support them when they attacked the city. Admiral Phipps' navy arrived much earlier than expected and so they waited for the rest of the troops to arrive. As he waited, Phipps noticed that statues of various saints adorned the towers of a nearby cathedral, and he became irritable. In his mood, he commanded his men to shoot at the statues with the ships' cannons. There is no record of how successful their target shooting was, but when the British land forces arrived and the signal was given to attack, Admiral Phipps was of no help at all. His men had used up all of the ships' ammunition on shooting at the "saints."

This story would be hilarious, if it weren't so tragic. Sometimes our Christian fellowship gets a little prickly because we have forgotten who our real enemies are. When we start to turn on each other in the church, we need to be reminded that there is another battle raging outside of the church property. I think the devil is quite happy to allow us to spend time and energy fighting against each other, because it means that we are not united in our struggle against him. Perhaps our churches need a little struggle from the outside that can bring us all back together to regroup and gather the right perspective.

Lawrence Richards comments that "while we may not appreciate the importance of Christian fellowship, until persecution comes, support from other believers is important at all times."[44] As I write this chapter, we are witnessing thousands of Christians facing persecution in Northern Iraq. They have been attacked by ISIS (The Islamic State) and are either being executed or forced to flee their cities.

Through all this tragedy a strange unity has developed in our local Christian communities. Instead of spending time squabbling over petty issues, we have seen a greater unity in our church fellowships. Believers have re-discovered that we are not the enemy and that by fighting with each other, we are "shooting the saints". When the real battle arrives we don't have any ammunition to fight, because we have shot it all at the other believers around us.

Within our Church community we have had to navigate through a few prickly issues over the past decades. In my time serving at our church, perhaps the most sensitive issue was over whether we should move our sanctuary into a bigger venue, which happened to be our church hall. It took numerous meetings and discussions to eventually make a decision, but in the end we did what we felt was the best for the Kingdom of God. Of course, the decision of the leadership wasn't unanimously received. However, I have to say that the members who had felt differently were gracious enough to move forward and to deal with their disappointment. In the end, our Church family was not permanently split over this issue and I thank God for his hand in leading us through that tricky decision.

The greater Church hasn't always been so fortunate in dealing with her issues of conflict. In 1054 the Western and Eastern churches officially spilt into two separate churches. Trouble had been brewing for hundreds of years, but eventually there was just too much division, doctrinal squabbles and animosity between the leadership, that the 'One' church sadly became 'Two.' In some ways, this was the end of a united Church, as more and more splits developed out of these churches. We could argue that on one level, these splits have aided the spread of the Gospel, but it still leaves a trail of brokenness. Often the divisions in our Church lead too much finger-pointing from other faith groups.

David Watson has been so bold as to declare that the over 9000 Christian denominations (and counting), throughout the world, is an insult to Christ. [45] I feel he has a valid point. Sure, we could argue that the more churches and denominations there are, the more the gospel can spread, but in truth this is not the case. Our witness is diminished as we spend valuable time and energy arguing with the broader Body of Christ. We are so obsessed with proving that our doctrine is better than another church, that we carry on like kids on a school playground, the world cries for a solution, a Saviour.

To put it simply - our struggle to fellowship with other Christians is a great slight on Jesus' call for unity, which we read about in John's gospel.

> "My prayer is not for them alone. I pray also for those who will believe in me through their message, [21] that all of them may be one, Father, just as you are in me and I am in you. May they also be in us so that the world may believe that you have sent me. [22] I have given them the glory that you gave me, that they may be one as we are one— I in them and you in me—so that they may be brought to complete unity. Then the world will know that you sent me and have loved them even as you have loved me." (John 17:20-23)

The other day I noticed a spider and a ladybird clinging to the Kreepy Crawly in the swimming pool. They were both desperate to get out of the pool and were doing all they could to avoid the ripples washing over them. Although I was aware of them, I am not sure they were aware of each other, or perhaps they didn't really care. I proceeded to watch the spider crawl all over the ladybird – he climbed over her back just to get to a better position on the pipe. I played the hero and rescued them both from the pool (ladybird first, as she had footprints on her back). As I put them on the side of the pool I thought to myself – Is that how we treat each other? Do we walk all over each other, just to get ourselves into a better position or a better job or a better self-image? Do we blatantly do *whatever it takes* just to pacify our selfish goals or because we feel our needs are more pressing than yours? It's worth thinking about!

We are urged to guard our witness and that the world will know that we are Christians, by our love. Yet, we easily do *whatever it takes* to destroy one another and to jealously guard our own doctrine or Church stance.

2.   *Our Personal Integrity*

There is a second reason why I believe we need to do *whatever it takes* to ensure godly fellowship in our communities. This reason has to do with our personal integrity. Just as I feel the witness of the church is at stake, so I believe that our individual integrity is also at stake. To explain what I mean, let's read the following words from John:

"If anyone says, 'I love God, 'yet hates his brother, he is a liar. For anyone who does not love his brother, whom he has seen, cannot love God, whom he has not seen. And he has given us this command: whoever loves God must also love his brother" (1 John 4:20-21).

So the Bible seems clear on this issue. I can't claim to 'love God', if I actually don't love you. I am actually a liar if I try and get away with this. My love for God is tightly linked into my fellowship with you. There are many people who claim to worship God on a Sunday, but who hate people in the family of God. This is a total contradiction and we fool ourselves if we think otherwise.

We can't always agree or think the same as each other, but the love of Jesus Christ should be our reference point. Sadly our fellowship in the church is often like this next poem:

Believe as I believe; no more, no less;
That I am right (and no one else) confess.
Feel as I feel, think only as I think;
Eat what I eat, and drink but what I drink.
Look as I look, do always as I do;
And then; and only then;
I'll fellowship with you.

We falsely believe that unity means we all have to agree. We assume that we can't enjoy fellowship with someone who thinks differently on a particular issue or who has another theological take on a topic. In his book, *The Pursuit of God*, A.W.Tozer challenges this notion, when he says:

> "Has it ever occurred to you that one hundred pianos all tuned to the same fork are automatically tuned to each other? They are of one accord by being tuned, not to each other, but to another standard to which each one must individually bow. So one hundred worshipers [meeting] together, each one looking away to Christ, are in heart nearer to each other than they could possibly be, were they to become 'unity' conscious and turn their eyes away from God to strive for closer fellowship."

I have also come to realise that proximity is not an indication of a healthy relationship. Being physically close to someone is no guarantee that we are living in a healthy relationship with that person. We just need to look at thousands of couples living in the same household, but who aren't able to get along. The same can be said about children and parents living under the same roof or even scholars sharing a classroom. We may be in the same proximity, but our relationships could be explosive.

When I worked outside of the Church context, I once shared an office with someone who I struggled to get along with. We sat in the same room, day in and day out, but I can honestly say our friendship wasn't great. I have seen the same scenario play out in the church context. There have been believers who belong to same home group, but who struggle to see eye to eye. Being in the same room as someone is never a guarantee of a healthy relationship.

"Being physically close to someone is no guarantee that we are living in a healthy relationship"

If we think about the story of the rich young ruler (Luke 18:18-30) for a moment, we note that he got physically close to Jesus, even speaking one on one with him, but he still didn't change his life. The Pharisees were the same. They got close to Jesus on numerous occasions, but this never meant that they embraced his teachings. Jacob and Esau lived in the same household, but their relationship was non-existent. David played the harp for King Saul, but Saul wanted to kill him. I think you get the point – we should never assume that just because we may be in the same proximity as someone, that our relationship is fine.

Dealing with Law and Grace in Christian Fellowship

The Church is not exempt from legalism and from believers who seem to be hell-bent on doing *whatever it takes* to make life a misery for the rest of the Body of Christ. Charles Swindoll tells the story of a young missionary couple who abandoned their ministry because their fellow missionaries had made their life 'hell'. The big issue that caused all the trouble was over a jar of peanut butter. That's right, your eyes haven't failed you – it was over a jar of delicious peanut butter. This is Swindoll's account of the story:

> "The particular place they were sent to serve the Lord did not have access to peanut butter. This family happened to enjoy peanut butter a great deal. Rather creatively, they made arrangements with some of their friends in the States to send them peanut butter every now and then so they could enjoy it with their meals. The problem was they didn't know until they started receiving the supply of peanut butter that the other missionaries considered it a mark of spirituality that you not have peanut butter with meals. I suppose the line went something like this: "We believe since we can't get peanut butter here, we should give it up for the cause of Christ," or some such nonsense. A basis of spirituality was "bearing the cross" of living without peanut butter...
>
> ...the legalism was so petty, the pressure got so intense and the exclusive treatment became so unfair, it finished them off spiritually. They finally had enough." [46]

I am still shaking my head at that story. It is not that I am surprised, it is just the insanity of the situation. Here was a family willing to give up their comfortable lifestyle in a First World country (except of course for the occasional jar of peanut butter) and to do what it takes to preach the Gospel, yet they faced opposition from people within the same missionary organisation. Their goal seemed to be: do *whatever it takes* to make this new family feel alienated and alone. Wow, that's absurd!

It was Jesus who offered new insight into the law. When He had an expert in the law ask him questions about eternal life, Jesus replies.

"What is written in the Law? How do you read it?"

The expert in the law answered: "Love the Lord your God with all your heart and with all your soul and with all your strength and with all your mind; and 'Love your neighbour as yourself."

"You have answered correctly," Jesus replied. "Do this and you will live." –
(Luke 10:26-28)

Following Jesus is about finding the balance of obeying the law and loving God and my neighbour. Too often our fellowship in our churches is flaky because we concentrate more on the laws and less on love. The following story may illustrate this point further.

Elisabeth Elliot writes about a young man who is eager to do whatever it takes to follow Christ. He asks the question, 'What is it I must forsake?' She records the following response in *The Liberty of Obedience* and shows how easily we misinterpret the cost of following Jesus.

> "You must give up coloured clothes, for one thing. Get rid of everything in your wardrobe that is not white. Stop sleeping on a soft pillow. Sell your musical instruments and don't eat anymore white bread. If you are sincere about obeying Christ you can't take warm baths, or shave your beard. To shave is to lie against Him who created us, to attempt to improve his work." [47]

Wow, I feel like a real sinner now. I fail in every one of those requirements. This legalistic approach to following Jesus sounds crazy to us, but this was the answer given in most Christian schools of the second century. When people ask us what it means to follow Jesus what rules do we make up in order to prove our piety. It is possible that the 'whatever it takes' mentality of today's church may seem out dated to the next generations. This is why I sincerely believe we need to tell people about Jesus, not our man-made ways of understanding him.

Christian fellowship is not all fun and games. There are some hard moments where we have to choose to 'love each other deeply.' These are the words of Peter:

"Above all, love each other deeply." – 1 Peter 4:7-10

Yet, how many times have we caught ourselves thinking…

- How am I supposed to 'love others' when I can't stand the person who sits on the other side of the church?
- Or how can I be friendly to that person who disagreed with me on that particular issue?
- How can I love those young people at church who look all weird?
- How can I love those old folks who think that their songs are better than mine?
- Does God really expect me to love that person who is so stubborn and unfriendly?

Paul urges us to try to look beyond our own needs and to look to the needs of others. "Do nothing out of selfish ambition or vain conceit. Rather, in humility value others above yourselves, not looking to your own interests but each of you to the interests of the others" (Philippians 2:3-4).

I have written a fair amount now on trying to maintain fellowship and unity in our church community, but what happens when it doesn't work? What do we do when our best efforts fall on deaf ears and people are still hell-bent on allowing divisions to persist? Well, we simply have to allow God to work things out. It may even mean choosing to hold your tongue for a while and to keep praying into that situation. It is also good to remind ourselves that God promised that He would build His church (and not us), so we can hand these troubles over to God.

John Oswalt adds, "we should, of course, live courageously and self-forgetfully, knowing that the church will survive. Furthermore, we should not be discouraged when difficulties come. Whether we deserve them or not, God's good purpose is not to destroy us but to purify us." [48]

If you are busy reading this chapter and you have stepped away from Christian fellowship for some reason, I urge you to make an effort to get connected again. I recognise that you may have justifiable grounds for disappointment in the church, but fellowship is vital to your Christian growth. I am convinced that we can't be disciples on our own. Gordon Cosby puts it in a better way, "for the most part, we are terribly isolated from people and we remain in a defensive stance toward those with whom we come in contact. To be alienated from people is to be alienated from God."

There is unique power in the community of faith. Belonging to the family of God is not only a privilege, but also a great responsibility. We are urged to show the world our Saviour and to reveal the power of the living God. The God we worship is not small and insignificant. The message we hold in our hearts is so powerful it can change lives. Sadly we often forget this when we are busy arguing over petty issues.

Annie Dillard once remarked, "on the whole, I do not find Christians, outside of the catacombs, sufficiently sensible of conditions. Does anyone have the foggiest idea what sort of power we so blithely invoke? The churches are children playing on the floor with their chemistry sets, mixing up a batch of TNT to kill a Sunday morning. It is madness to wear ladies' straw hats and velvet hats to church; we should all be wearing crash helmets. Ushers should issue life preservers and signal flares; they should lash us to our pews." [49]

To stress this point further, Calvin Miller, in his book *The Table of Inwardness*, writes of an antique wooden box that was stored in his home. The box had been specifically made to store dynamite, especially when it was in transit from the manufacturer to its new home. On the top of the box, in big letters, were written 'Danger Dynamite!' One day Miller looked inside the dusty box and saw that it had now been filled with ordinary bits and pieces. In a moment of inspiration he realised that this is what many weary Christ-followers now feel and look like. We are made to house the Spirit of the Living God – to be dynamic and alive, yet we find ourselves occupied with all sorts of junk! [50]

So, think about your community and especially your own church for a moment. Is there some strain in your fellowship group or with someone at your church? Remember we are the ones called to do *whatever it takes* to bridge this brokenness. We can't just let it continue to fester without trying to urge unity and true fellowship!

TIME OF REFLECTION

As you move onto the next chapter, I ask you to pray through these questions.

1. Has someone in your church community hurt you? Will you offer them forgiveness and grace or are you wanting to hold onto your grudge a little longer?

2. What does this verse challenge you to do?

Acts 2:42 - They devoted themselves to the apostles' teaching and to the fellowship, to the breaking of bread and to prayer.

If you answered 'yes' to this previous questions, is it not time then to challenge yourself to go a little deeper with Christ? How will you do that?

3.   Pray for unity in your spiritual home. Perhaps you could use Psalm 133 as a starting point.

How good and pleasant it is
  when God's people live together in unity!
It is like precious oil poured on the head,
  running down on the beard,
running down on Aaron's beard,
  down on the collar of his robe.
It is as if the dew of Hermon
  were falling on Mount Zion.
For there the LORD bestows his blessing,
  even life forevermore.

4.   My friend Michael Cassidy wrote a wonderful book, *The Church Jesus prayed for*, which is based on John 17. Try and get a copy of it if you can, but in the meantime read John 17 and note what Jesus has to say on unity.

ten

FINAL WORD

MAKING THINGS CRYSTAL CLEAR

"Don't let your learning lead to knowledge; let your learning lead to action."

- JIM ROHN

"If we want to know how much God loves us, Calvary gives the answer. He loves us to the very end."

- MICHAEL CASSIDY

If you have ever visited the Mort Docks in Sydney, Australia, then you will know the story of Thomas Mort. As a 19th Century explorer Thomas noticed that there was a major problem with transporting meat from Australia to Britain. The main issue was poor refrigeration and as a result so much meat went bad before it arrived in Europe.

Thomas Mort gave himself the goal of sorting out this dilemma in just 3 years, which seemed a little ambitious at the time. In the end, it didn't take him 3, 10 or even 15 years. It ended up taking him 26 years! He lived just long enough to see the first shipment of refrigerated meat leave Sydney and arrive 'fresh' in Britain.

What a wonderful story of perseverance – Thomas Mort surely lived out a *whatever it takes* attitude. The house that Thomas lived in still stands in Sydney today and if you visit this home you should take note of something profound. If you look at the cornice of the study ceiling, you will see the following words painted over 20 times on the ceiling:

"To persevere is to succeed."

Whatever it takes will always mean perseverance. We may not get it right the first time or even the tenth time, but if we are willing to persevere then we can go a long way. I believe that God is looking for men and women, young and old, who are willing to persevere until the end. A call has been sounded, but few are willing to respond to God's plea:

"I looked for a person among them who would build up the wall and stand before me in the gap on behalf of the land." – Ezekiel 22:30

In his book *Stand in the Gap*, David Bryant challenges us to live a *whatever it takes* lifestyle in the presence of God. He says, 'to stand in the gap means to place no limits on how fully God may use you, or for whose sake. It means that, as God directs you, you are willing to take on any role, any time, any place, by any means, with anyone and at any cost that will help close the gap..." [51]

Imagine for a moment that you are going on a much anticipated camping holiday at the beach. You have been preparing for this for ages and so you head off in great excitement. The caravan is packed, the tents are ready and the bikes are on the racks. A few kilometres down the highway you see a sign board that indicates 'Durban 60 km' to go. So believing you are already at your destination you pull over and set up your Caravan and tents. After all the sign does say Durban doesn't it? You get a few strange looks from people as they speed past your campsite next to the road sign, but you seem happy enough and they carry on to their destinations.

Of course we are neglecting to read the most crucial part of the sign – the actual distance still to go to your destination! Durban is 60 km's away and you have not arrived there yet. Many of us fall into the trap of thinking that we have already arrived. We are too busy living life 'under a signpost', when we need to push on until we reach our actual destination.

Karl Barth uses a similar analogy to describe the decisions of the Israelites. On their journey they find a sign pointing westward – this signpost is there to point them to their destination, but instead they stop and create a life for themselves under its painted words.

> "They built a civilisation there, celebrating the signpost and telling stories of how they arrived at the marker. Rituals evolve and songs are written. Books are published and liturgies follow. A few travel on and return, confirming that the sign does indeed lead to the place promised. But the second and third generations have built a life around the signpost and have forgotten the meaning of the journey. Their life is built on stories of past travel, not on stories of arriving or on the prophetic call to get on with the journey themselves." [52]

Being the kind of person that is willing to lead a *whatever it takes* lifestyle means that we need to accept we have never arrived. There will always be more. Jesus' call will bring new challenges on a daily basis. There will always be trouble, hardship and issues to face. However, if we hold close to our hearts that God has already done everything to provide for our salvation, victory is already assured. We are asked to walk the path of faithfulness and to do *whatever it takes* to remain true to our Saviour.

"We are asked to walk the path of faithfulness and to do whatever it takes to remain true to our Saviour."

I am ready to say today, "You can count me in."

How about you?

I discovered the other day that the word disaster comes from the Latin word meaning 'to be disconnected from the stars?' I find that fascinating. I love standing beneath the stars on a glorious winter's evening. They seem so clear and bright, but also so distant. Richard Rohr contemplates that "the stars represented the great story, the universal story. Our lives are usually a disaster unless we live under these stars. We live our little story under the great story." [53]

This great story is the story of God's creation and then His ultimate redemption of human kind. It is the story of God's willingness to love us even when we weren't lovable. I am sure that my life would be a 'disaster' if I remained disconnected from the 'Great Story' of Jesus. And so, I resolve to do what it takes to avert this isolation and disconnection.

People say that when Abraham Lincoln's body was brought from Washington to Illinois, it passed through the small town of Albany. As he was carried through the streets a young mother and her son stood and watched the procession. As the crowd came nearer to where she was standing, this young woman lifted her son as far as she could reach above the heads of the crowd. She urged him to look at the body of the great President, saying to her bewildered son, "Take a long look, my boy. He died for you".

Perhaps today we need to lift our spirits to see Calvary. As we take a long look at Jesus, let us remember that He died for us. If Jesus died for us, then surely we should be willing to live for him?

The Father was willing to do *whatever it takes* to get us back into a right relationship with Himself. He was willing to pay for our sins and that meant watching his own son die at the hands of people who hated him. Jesus was willing to do *whatever it takes* to offer us hope and salvation. This meant facing shame, ridicule and rejection – all for your sake and mine. There is a saying that goes, "Fidel a la Mort", which means "Faithful unto death." These three words summarize the heart and soul of Jesus. He was willing to be faithful to His father's plan – faithful even unto death.

I remember as a child having a book on many famous adventurers and explorers. I used to read it over and over again. The book included stories of Christopher Columbus, Vasco Da Gama, David Livingstone, Ferdinand Magellan and they all filled my sleep with dreams of great adventures.

These explorers were prepared to do *whatever it takes* to satisfy their insatiable desire to discover new worlds. Even in our modern era, we would still find it a daunting task to head off to some distant shore on a rickety wooden ship, even if we had our GPS with us. In the days of these explorers it was a monumental decision to head off from the safety of your country into the unknown. The world was supposed to be flat, the oceans were filled with dragons, serpents, leviathans and other monsters. If they didn't get you first, then you were bound to fall off the end of the earth. However, these explorers believed in something else – they hoped that there was more and they were willing to do *whatever it takes* to find it.

There is a part of Christopher Columbus' journey to America that inspires me. As an Italian living in Spain, he found support for his mission to find a short cut to the East Indies, from an unlikely source. King Ferdinand and Queen Isabella supplied him with the money and ships necessary to start his voyage of discovery. After months of sailing they had found no land and his sailors were ready to turn around and go home (I am surprised they put up with it for so long, in the first place). After hearing the constant nagging of his crew, Columbus said to them, "3 more days. Then if we don't find land we will turn around and go back home."

On the second day, they sighted land and 'discovered' the island now known as San Salvador. When you set your mind on doing *whatever it takes,* you need to be prepared to go a little further than the next person. We can't just give up when the pressure mounts and the voices urge us to stop. If God has called you to do something for him, then we need to be prepared to do *whatever it takes.*

William Borden was a wealthy Christian growing up in Chicago as an heir of the Borden milk fortune. When he was in his first year at Yale University he committed himself to reaching out to the Muslim community in Northern India. A few years later he set sail for Egypt where he had chosen to study Arabic as part of his preparation before heading off to India. William knew that money would not buy security in the long run, so he courageously gave away his inheritance to various mission organisations.

He had only been in Egypt for four months when he mysterious contracted spinal meningitis. William fought the disease bravely, but he died within a few weeks. When his body was removed from his room, friends found a note that he had scrawled on a piece of paper. He had hidden the note under his pillow. The words read,

"No reserve! No retreat! No regrets!"

If we want to live a lifestyle that embraces the *whatever it takes* spirit then we need to give as much as William Borden chose to give.

No reserve!

No retreat!

No regrets!

Jeremiah was a *whatever it takes* kind of prophet, even though he would probably tell us otherwise. He tried to squirm his way out of his calling, but God wouldn't have any of his nonsense. In the end, Jeremiah spoke the truth boldly, and when it got him into trouble, he turned to the Lord for help and strength. Eugene Peterson makes an interesting remark about Jeremiah's long 23 years of suffering:

"Jeremiah did not resolve to stick it out for 23 years, no matter what; he got up every morning with the sun. The day was God's day, not the people's day. He didn't get up to face rejection; he got up to meet with God. He didn't rise to put up with another round of mocking; he rose to be with the Lord. That is the secret of his persevering pilgrimage – not thinking with dread about the long road ahead, but greeting the present moment, every present moment, with obedient delight, with expectant hope: "my heart is ready!"" [54]

I am convinced that we will never live fully for God unless we can say, "my heart is ready."

So, let me ask us again. Are you now willing to do *whatever it takes*...

To follow Jesus?

To restore your relationships?

To build a bridge in your friendships?

To love those who irritate you?

To fight for the unity of the Body of Christ?

WHATEVER IT TAKES

To worship, praise and love the God who died for us?

As we conclude this book, I would like to offer you the following prayer, written by Charles de Foucauld. It is well worth praying ourselves and so I invite you to find a quiet place and pray this prayer.

"Father, I abandon myself into your hands;
Do with me what you will.
What you may do, I thank you;
I am ready for all, I accept all,
Let only your will be done in me,
And in all your creatures –
I wish no more than this,
O Lord."

Thanks again for taking the time to journey with me. May God bless you.

Do *whatever it takes!*

Living in Grace

Delme

eleven

FINDING COURAGE

STORIES TO INSPIRE US TO DO WHATEVER IT TAKES

"It is a dangerous thing – a very dangerous thing – to have a skimpy impression of the Almighty God."

- GORDON MACDONALD

"Courage is the capacity to live constantly with our deepest beliefs, no matter what confronts us. It is steadfastly holding on to what we put first and standing by it in every circumstance."

- TREVOR HUDSON

My Christian faith has been shaped by many amazing people over the past four decades. Most of them continue to be my mentors, role models and fellow Christians on this journey of faith. I am so grateful for their faithfulness along the way and I will always be indebted to them for pointing me in the right direction.

There are equally a large number of our Christian ancestors who have been witnesses to me, yet I have never met any of them. Their stories inspire me to be the kind of believer who is willing to do *whatever it takes*. So the last chapter of this book is a collection of the brief stories of just ten of these men and women. Of course, I could have chosen many more than these ten (including some well-known figures), but this is not meant to be an exhaustive list. Your list may have ten completely different names on it, but I offer you my list to help us all find courage.

All of these individuals have embodied the *whatever it takes* spirit in their lives and it is my prayer that you would be encouraged and challenged by their brief stories. Becoming a *whatever it takes* Christ follower is all about courage. As Nelson Mandela once said,

"I learned that courage was not the absence of fear, but the triumph over it. The brave man is not he who does not feel afraid, but he who conquers that fear."

The Bible also mentions a list of heroes of faith. Some of these names are well known and impressive, including Abraham, Enoch, Moses, David, Joseph, Isaac and even Rahab. What stands out about these people was that they were willing to 'find courage' even when things looked bleak for them. As Paul writes, "all these people were still living by faith when they died. They did not receive the things promised; they only saw them and welcomed them from a distance, admitting that they were foreigners and strangers on earth" (Hebrews 11:13).

Each of the following ten Christ-followers deserves a whole book reflecting on their lives and many libraries already contain their complete stories. However, it is not my intention in this chapter to write a comprehensive biography on each of them. My purpose is to introduce you to these ten dynamic people, who have in some way, shaped my spiritual life. I have purposefully kept this brief and have added a few meaningful quotes from each of these inspiring people. It is my prayer and hope that you may be inspired and encouraged by their stories.

Perhaps the best way to reflect on each of these incredible people is to read their stories and then to pause for a few minutes. Allow the information and 'spirit' of their lives to form a prayer in your heart. It may be helpful to then pray that prayer and journal some thoughts before moving onto the next person of courage.

1.   Perpetua (185-211)

The first time I heard Perpetua's story I was overwhelmed by her courage and commitment to Christ. Much against her father's wishes Perpetua committed her life to Christ around the year 203 A.D. Choosing to become a follower of Christ was not an easy choice to make in the age of Roman rule, especially under the vicious Septimus Severus. It spelt certain persecution and even death, which explains why her father tried his best to dissuade her from serving Jesus. As a noblewoman, Perpetua had everything going for her, but it seemed she was willing to give it all up for the sake of her faith in Jesus.

Along with her companion and servant, Felicity, Perpetua was arrested for her faith and sent to prison. Perpetua was still nursing a young child at the time of her arrest and Felicity was eight months pregnant. Days after Felicity gave birth to her child, both her and Perpetua were led out into the Amphitheatre and were ripped apart by wild animals.

It was hoped that a gory death would dissuade others from following Jesus, but the witness of Perpetua and Felicity served to galvanise the resolve of the believers of the early third century. Both of these brave women were willing to do *whatever it takes* for Christ. I salute their bravery and witness. It is said that Perpetua's last words were: *"Stand fast in the faith and love one another."*

"It will all happen in the prisoner's dock as God wills, for you may be sure that we are not left to ourselves but are all in His power." – Perpetua

2.   John Wycliffe (1320– 1384)

Martin Luther gets a lot of deserved credit for the Reformation, but we don't often hear of the men and women who laid the ground work for the spread of these new ideas. I remind my Church History students that it takes a unique person to change the course of history, but often these people stand on the shoulders of those who have gone before them. Many pre-reformers had already been challenging the status quo for decades before Luther was even born. One of these brave people was John Wycliffe.

Wycliffe was a highly educated man, becoming a Doctor of Theology through Oxford University. Around the year 1374 A.D., Wycliffe spoke out against the sale of indulgences and verbally chastised the Pope. Obviously this didn't go down well in Rome and the Pope issued five decrees against John, condemning him on nineteen different charges.

However, this didn't stop Wycliffe from speaking his mind and he later opposed other ideas and doctrines of the Church. The troubles that came with his outspoken theology forced him to retire from public life, which ultimately allowed him the time to accomplish something truly remarkable.

Wycliffe translated the Bible into English for the very first time. This English translation made the Scriptures available to the ordinary people of England. The people who could read were able to tell other people what the Bible actually said, instead of relying on the interpretation of the priests.

Wycliffe and his followers went out amongst ordinary people of the land and preached the gospel to them in a language they could understand. His followers were known as Lollard's and their influence continued even after the death of Wycliffe in 1384 A.D.

John had irked the Church establishment so much that forty years after his death; his bones were dug up and burnt by order of the Pope. When you live a life fully committed to Christ, you will often end up rocking the boat and making enemies for yourself. Despite all the resistance he faced, John Wycliffe was always willing to do *whatever it takes* in order to follow Jesus. The following quotes are attributed to him:

"I believe that in the end the truth will conquer."

"The laity ought to understand the faith, and since the doctrines of our faith are in the Scriptures, believers should have the Scriptures in a language familiar to the people...."

3.   Julian of Norwich (1342 - 1416)

Julian of Norwich was a fourteenth century English Mystic who, in her later life, chose to live as a recluse (also known as an Anchoress). Her desire was to give everything up for Jesus and to live a simple life. She had a stone cell built into the side wall of a church so that she could spend all her time in prayer and worship. This church is now known as the Church of St. Julian.

Little is known of her early life, but scholars suggest that when she was about thirty years old Julian fell very ill. While on her death bed, in the May of 1343 AD, she received a number of visions from God, which she referred to as 'showings'. She later wrote these down in a book entitled *Sixteen Revelations of Divine Love.*

These moments with God proved to be her true conversion experience and prompted her to become a recluse, giving her entire life to Christ. Her choice was not an easy one, but she felt that this was her way of being able to do *whatever it takes* for Jesus. She became one the leading Mystics of all time and she influenced many believers of her generation.

Her legacy lives on in the witness of many faithful Christ-followers and is even written in the poem by T.S. Eliot, *Little Gidding.* These are her words, recorded in that poem:

"All shall be well, and all shall be well, and all manner of thing shall be well."

This prayer is also attributed to Julian:

"God, of your goodness, give me yourself; you are enough for me, and anything less

that I could ask for would not do you full honour. And if I ask anything that is less, I shall always lack something, but in you alone I have everything."

4. Thomas a Kempis (1380 – 1471)

I can't seem to get enough of the writings of Thomas a Kempis. Besides the Holy Bible, Thomas' book *The Imitation of Christ* is the work that I have read and studied the most. Up until recent history this book was the second most popular piece of Christian literature, next to the Bible of course. If you have never read it, let me urge you to get your hands on a copy – it may just change your life.

Thomas was born in Kempen, Germany and was the second child of John and Gertrude Haemerken. As a young man he was sent to Deventer, in the Netherlands, to study under the guidance of the Brethren of Common Life. This community became synonymous with a modern form of devotion, which we now know as the *Devotio Moderna* (modern devotion). The practise of their spirituality was life changing for Thomas and under the strong mentorship of people like Gerhard Groote, Thomas dedicated his life to their movement, becoming an effective priest and writer.

One of the remarkable things of his life is that he remained in the same monastery for nearly 70 years. It was in Mount St Agnes that he devoted his time to prayer, study, copying manuscripts, teaching, writing and also hearing the confessions of people who came to the monastery.

It was the custom of the Brothers of Common Life to collect wise sayings on various spiritual matters and then to practise them and learn them. It is thought that the book *The Imitation of Christ* was compiled by Thomas, but was greatly influence by the community in which he served.

His life may seem ordinary compared to other well-known Christian figures, but his decision to write *The Imitation of Christ* left a massive legacy for the Christian movement. His writings greatly influenced people like Martin Luther, John Calvin and John Wesley. It could be argued that without the influence of Thomas a Kempis, Germany, France and England would be very different countries today.

There is so much I could say about this inspiring person, but I will leave you to discover more of his works by yourself. To end with, here are a few wise words from my friend, Thomas a Kempis:

"Without the way, there is no going;
Without the truth, there is no knowing;
Without the life, there is no living."

"Love flies, runs, leaps for joy; it is free and unrestrained.
Love gives all for all, resting in One who is highest above all things,
from whom every good flows and proceeds." [55]

5.   Anne Askew (1520 – 1546)

"I said that I would rather die than break my faith."- Anne Askew

Anne Askew was an English poet who died as a martyr at just 26 years old. History records that Anne was first tortured in the Tower of London and then burnt at the stake. At 15 she was forced to marry to Thomas Kyme, but because of her strong Protestant views Thomas kicked her out of their family home.

Anne reverted back to her family name of Askew and she continued to share her faith within the city of London. Soon rumours surfaced that she had been speaking to Queen Catherine of her faith and this angered the King's Court. It is thought that King Henry VIII heard of this and had Anne arrested. She was later tortured for her different Christian beliefs, which were considered "heretical" at the time. She remained completely loyal to Queen Catherine and remained silent when she was repeatedly asked whether Catherine also believed in the Protestant ideas.

On the 16 July 1546 Anne was burnt at the stake. Scholars say that she was carried to her execution in a chair as her hours of torture on the rack had left her unable to walk. Due to her unwillingness to recant from her understanding of Christ, Anne was slowly burnt alive rather than being strangled first. Those who saw her execution were impressed by her bravery.

Even until her dying breath she refused to turn her back on Jesus Christ. In my mind, she was willing to do *whatever it takes* for her Lord, no matter the cost. The following words are attributed to Anne:

"O Lord, I have more enemies now, than there be hairs on my head! Yet, Lord, let them never overcome me with vain words, but fight thou, Lord, in my stead: for on Thee cast I my care! With all the spite they can imagine, they fall upon me, who am Thy poor creature. Yet, sweet Lord, let me not set by them that are against me; for in Thee is my whole delight. And, Lord, I heartily desire of Thee, that, Thou wilt, of Thy most merciful goodness, forgive them that violence which they do, and have done unto me."

I am inspired by her absolute commitment to the cause of Christ. Even though her death came at the hands of fellow 'Christians' she never blamed God for her torture and arrest. She always remained focussed on preaching the essence of Jesus Christ and she paid the ultimate price for her beliefs.

John Foxe wrote these words as a testimony to the courage of Anne:

"The good Anne Askew ... being compassed in with the flames of fire, as a blessed sacrifice unto God... leaving behind her a singular example of Christian constancy for all men to follow."

6.   C.S. Lewis (1899-1963)

Clive Staples Lewis was born in 1899 in Belfast, Northern Ireland. His mother died when he was just ten years old and this may have driven Clive to retreat into a world of books. He showed incredible signs of promise and giftedness, winning a scholarship to Oxford University in 1916. Unfortunately he wasn't able to study immediately as he was sent to fight in the Somme valley in France, during the First World War. He was wounded during the war and after a lengthy recovery returned to Oxford to study.

It was during 1931 that C.S. Lewis became a Christ-follower and it was this decision that shaped all of his subsequent writings. He is well known for his series of books, *The Chronicles of Narnia,* as well as many other Christian works, including *Mere Christianity, The Screwtape Letters, Surprise by Joy, The Problem of Pain* and *The Great Divorce.*

Lewis married Joy Gresham in 1956 even though she was already ill with cancer at the time. Joy initially recovered but four years later the cancer returned and she passed away. Lewis wrote an account of his struggle with Joy's death entitled *A Grief Observed* and their story was made into a movie entitled *Shadowlands.*

When I read *The Chronicles of Narnia* to my children I am amazed at how the works of C.S. Lewis have impacted so many lives. He will be remembered as more than just a writer, but also as an apologist, a poet, a novelist and a devoted follower of Jesus. Clive Staple Lewis was willing to do *whatever it takes* to follow Jesus and the following quotes reflect his faith.

- *"I believe in Christianity as I believe that the sun has risen: not only because I see it, but because by it I see everything else."*

- *"God cannot give us a happiness and peace apart from Himself, because it is not there. There is no such thing."*

7.   Jim Elliot (1927-1956)

I first came across the name of Jim Elliot when I was in my early twenties. At the time I knew nothing of his life's story, but it was the following words that left an indelible mark on my life:

- *"He is no fool who gives what he cannot keep to gain that which he cannot lose."*

Even from a young age Jim Elliot had a passion to serve God. In 1952 when the opportunity came around for Jim to work amongst the Quichuas people, in Ecuador, he grabbed it with both hands. For more than three years Jim worked with other missionaries amongst the Quichuas people, learning the local language and eventually establishing a missionary post in the community.

In 1955 Jim Elliot and his colleagues began their attempts to get to know another tribe in Ecuador, the Auca's. This tribe was even more mysterious than the Quichuas and despite early signs of a breakthrough, Elliot and his friends were brutally murdered a year later. Jim Elliot was just 29 years of age.

The unnecessary death of Jim and his friends seemed to destroy any hope of Christ being preached to the Auca people, but God had other plans. Jim's wife, Elisabeth and another young woman, Rachel Saint felt called to continue the work begun by the five brave men. They learnt the language of the Auca tribe and taught them about the forgiveness of Jesus. Soon these courageous women established a church among the Auca's and many of the tribe came to know the Lord.

It could have easily been concluded that Jim Elliot's dream had ended in complete failure, but thankfully God doesn't measure success like we do. Jim's death has become a world-wide testimony of faith in Christ and dedication to the work of God. His *whatever it takes* attitude has changed the lives of many people and even though his earthly life was cut short, his legacy lives on.

"I seek not a long life, but a full one, like you Lord Jesus."

"There is nothing worth living for, unless it is worth dying for." – Elisabeth Elliot

8.   Dietrich Bonhoeffer – (1906 – 1945)

Dietrich Bonhoeffer was born in Breslau, Germany in 1906. Although his family were not too religious, Dietrich surprised them all by announcing that he wanted to become a priest. He was just 14 years old when he broke the news to them. Dietrich followed through with his desire and was ultimately ordained as a priest in 1931.

Bonhoeffer lived in a great time of upheaval in Europe and especially in Germany. Adolf Hitler had just been elected chancellor of Germany in 1933 and while many people saw this as a positive sign, Bonhoeffer was not a fan of Hitler. He became a fierce opponent of Hitler's philosophy and was willing to go on national radio criticising Hitler, and in particular the danger of what seemed to be, an idolatrous cult of the Fuhrer.

Bonhoeffer opposed the persecution of the Jews, arguing that the Christian community had a responsibility to act against this kind of policy. He even tried his hardest to prevent the Nazi ideology from infiltrating the Protestant church. In the end this caused much division and led to a breakaway church, which became known as The Confessing Church.

Needless to say this all didn't go down to well with Hitler and his supporters. Dietrich Bonhoeffer was declared an enemy of the state, as well as an enemy of the Germany church. He was ultimately arrested and executed at the Flossian concentration camp in 1945. The tragedy was that he died just one month before the end of the war.

It is said that just before his execution, Dietrich asked a fellow inmate to pass on a message to Bishop George Bell of Chichester. This was the message:

'This is the end – for me the beginning of life.'

Dietrich Bonhoeffer is also revered as an author and a Theologian. One of his famous works is entitled *The Cost of Discipleship*, which is a study on the Sermon on the Mount. In this book he argues that we need greater spiritual discipline in the church and that we should never practise 'cheap grace'. God's grace came at a huge cost and so we should remember this as we seek to follow Jesus.

"Cheap grace is the grace we bestow on ourselves. Cheap grace is the preaching of forgiveness without requiring repentance, baptism without church discipline, Communion without confession.... Cheap grace is grace without discipleship, grace without the cross, grace without Jesus Christ, living and incarnate." [56]

- *"One act of obedience is better than one hundred sermons."*

9.   Keith Green – (1953 – 1982)

When I was 20 years old I was given a copy of Keith Green's biography *No Compromise* and I believe that in many ways it changed my life. I had never heard of Keith Green at the time, but realised that I had been singing some of his worship songs for years. His songs included *'There is a Redeemer'*, *'Create in me a clean heart'* and *'Oh Lord, You're beautiful.'*

Keith was a young man who was 'sold out' for Jesus and was willing to do whatever it takes to share the gospel through music. Just as the title of his biography suggests, Keith took his faith seriously and he was not willing to compromise anything of the Good News.

Even though he was a gifted musician, song writer and artist, he was willing to lay these talents down, if this was what God wanted from him. Thankfully, Keith discovered that God rather wanted him to channel his abilities in producing music that would glorify Jesus Christ. In the end, this has become Keith's ultimate Legacy. He died tragically, just short of his 30th birthday. Two of his children, Josiah (3) and Bethany (2) died alongside Keith as their plane crashed shortly after take-off.

Melody Green wrote her husband's biography in 1989, using his journal entries as the source of this remarkable story. It was appropriately titled *No Compromise* and clearly portrayed the *whatever it takes* attitude of Keith. The book also revealed the meaning that Keith found in Christ, which he so aptly sums up as:

"I repent of ever having recorded one single song, and ever having performed one concert, if my music, and more importantly, my life has not provoked you into Godly jealousy or to sell out more completely to Jesus!"

- *"If somebody writes a great poem, people don't run around applauding the pencil, saying 'Oh, what a great pencil'... I'm a pencil in God's hands."*

These are some of the words from his song 'Make my life a prayer to You.' –

"Make my life a prayer to You
I wanna do what you want me to
No empty words and no white lies
No token prayers no compromise."

10.   **Desmond Tutu – (1931 – present)**

In 1994 I completed my Bachelor of Commerce degree at the University of Kwazulu Natal (formerly known as Natal University). We were privileged to have Archbishop Desmond Tutu as the guest speaker at our Graduation ceremony, even though this was a very turbulent time in our country. A large number of the University graduates were white students and most of us had been fed many lies about Bishop Desmond Tutu.

So it was with a little uncertainty that we sat at our Graduation waiting for the address from Bishop Tutu. However, we needn't have worried as Desmond Tutu was absolutely brilliant. He had the entire gathering eating out of the palm of his hand and in so doing, began changing the mind-sets of thousands of people. I came away from that ceremony realising that I had been in the presence of a remarkable man of God.

Desmond Tutu was born in 1931 in the town of Klerksdorp, which is in the former Western Transvaal. Even though his family came from humble beginnings Tutu trained as a teacher and then, later, as a priest. He was ordained in 1960 and it was in his role as a priest that became an outspoken critic of Apartheid.

Tutu has experienced at first hand the incredible pain of our nation, walking alongside many families impacted by Apartheid and injustice, including the fateful Soweto uprising on 16 June 1976. Desmond was appointed as the Chairperson of the Truth and Reconciliation Commission (TRC) in 1995, which was set up to deal with the atrocities of the past. In order to be fully committed to this task, Tutu retired as the Archbishop of Cape Town as he wanted to devote all his time to the work of the TRC, thus offering healing and forgiveness to thousands of people impacted by Apartheid.

Desmond has been honoured with many awards and titles over his lifetime, including the Nobel Peace Prize in 1984 and then being ordained as the Archbishop of Cape Town, in 1986, becoming the first Black person to lead the Anglican Church of the Province of Southern Africa.

In all of his eighty plus years, Desmond has maintained his faith and his prophetic voice against all social and political ills. Although Tutu has officially retired from public life he continues to speak out on moral and political issues affecting South Africa and other countries around the world. He has even vocally criticised the new Government and ruling party when he has felt that they have fallen short of the democratic ideals which his contemporaries fought for. His *whatever it takes* attitude to life and Christianity has inspired many people and reminded us of the role of a Godly prophet.

Today Desmond Tutu is highly revered for his knowledge, views and experience, especially around the issue of reconciliation. It was Tutu who coined the phrase 'Rainbow Nation', which has been used effectively to promote harmony among all people of South Africa and I fully believe that his legacy will live on beyond his earthly life.

Here are just two of the many quotes attributed to Desmond Tutu.

- *Without forgiveness, there's no future.*

- *Hope is being able to see that there is light despite all of the darkness.*

Hebrews 11:32-40

32 And what more shall I say? I do not have time to tell about Gideon, Barak, Samson and Jephthah, about David and Samuel and the prophets, 33 who through faith conquered kingdoms, administered justice, and gained what was promised; who shut the mouths of lions, 34 quenched the fury of the flames, and escaped the edge of the sword; whose weakness was turned to strength; and who became powerful in battle and routed foreign armies. 35 Women received back their dead, raised to life again. There were others who were tortured, refusing to be released so that they might gain an even better resurrection. 36 Some faced jeers and flogging, and even chains and imprisonment. 37 They were put to death by stoning; they were sawed in two; they were killed by the sword. They went about in sheepskins and goatskins, destitute, persecuted and mistreated— 38 the world was not worthy of them. They wandered in deserts and mountains, living in caves and in holes in the ground. 39 These were all commended for their faith, yet none of them received what had been promised, 40 since God had planned something better for us so that only together with us would they be made perfect.

REFERENCES

1   Richard Rohr, *Jesus' plan for a new world*, St. Anthony messenger press, Ohio, 1996, pg.20

2   Don Marquis quote from www.donmarquis.com

3   Story of Mohamed Bouazizi - www.theguardian.com/world/2011/may/15/arab-spring-tunisia-the-slap

4   David Bryant, *Stand in the Gap*, Regal Books, California, 1997, pg.106

5   Floyd McClung, *Loving the God who loves you*, Kingsway Publications, Eastbourne, 1993, pg.154-155

6   William Wilberforce quote - www.goodreads.com

7   Geoffrey Canada – article from http://hcz.org/about-us/leadership/geoffrey-canada/

8   Howard Bell, *More than a Conqueror*, Treasure House, Shippensburg, 1997, pg.153

9   Gary Burke, The NIV Application Commentary: *Esther*, Zondervan Publishing, 1999, pg.139

10 Jars of Clay, *Worlds Apart*, released 1996.

11 Dennis Fisher, *Our Daily Bread*, 5 June 2011.

12 Richard Foster, *Longing for God*, Hodder and Stoughton, London, 2009, pg.112

13 AW Tozer quote from www.goodreads.com

14 John Oswalt, *The NIV Application commentary: Isaiah*, Zondervan, Michigan, pg.120

15 John Oswalt, *The NIV Application commentary: Isaiah*, Zondervan, Michigan.

16 Edgar Guest, *All That Matters*.

17 Zig Ziglar quotes from www.zigzlar.com

18 Alan Paton, *Instrument of Thy peace*, Fontana, December 1969.

19 William Barclay's commentary on *Hebrews*, page 108.

20 Quote from https://thecounselingmoment.wordpress.com/tag/first-epistle-of-peter/

21 Eugene Peterson from Matthew 6 in *The Message*.

22 Patrick Morley, 1996, *The Seasons of Rebuilding*, Lifeway Press, Nashville, pg.28.

23 C.S.Lewis quote from https://www.cslewis.com/blog/a-cancer-in-the-universe/

24 Barbara Johnson, 1992, *Splashes of Joy in the Cesspools of Life*, Word Publishing, Dallas, pg.176

25 Michael Cassidy, *Chasing the Wind*, African Enterprise, 2002, page 189.

26 Newspaper publication - www.sermonillustrations.com

27 Albert Drurer story from the *NIV Application Commentary*, edited by Gary Burke.

28 Gordon Macdonald, *Ordering Your Private World*.

29 Stephen Ambrose, *Band of Brothers*, Pocket Books, 2001.

30 John 15:13

31 John 15:15

32 1 Samuel 20

33 Psalm 41:9

34   Ecclesiastes 4:9-12

35   Derick Bingham, Encouragement: *Oxygen for the soul*, Christian Focus, 2001.

36   Henson Towne, *Around the Corner*.

37   Richard Wurmbrand, *My Correspondence with Jesus*, Monarch Publications, Eastbourne, 1990, pg.8.

38   Bilquis Sheikh, *I dared to call him Father*, Chosen Books, 2003.

39   Gordon MacDonald, *Forging a real world faith*, Highland books, 1990, pg.73.

40   P.P.Job, *Why God God?*, Tortured for Christ, 2000.

41   Good News Broadcaster, April 1985, p.12

42   Robert McGee, *The Search for Significance*, W.Publishing group, Nashville, pg.124.

43   James Packer, *Your Father Loves you*, Harold Shaw Publishers, 1986.

44   Sermon Illustrations, *Our Daily Bread*.

45   David Watson quote , Discipleship, Hodder and Stoughton, London, 1981pg 37

46   *Grace Awakening*, Charles Swindoll, Word Publishing, Dallas, 1990, page 93-94

47   Elisabeth Elliot, *The Liberty of Obedience*, 1968, pg32-33.

48   The NIV Application Commentary: *Isaiah*, Zondervan, 2003, pg.87

49   Annie Dillard, *Teaching a Stone to talk*, HarperCollins, 2009

50   Gordon MacDonald, *Restoring your Spiritual Passion*, pg.205

51   David Bryant, 1997, *Stand in the Gap*, Regal Books,

52   Gary Burke, 2000, *The NIV Application commentary*, Zondervan Publishing, Michigan, pg.268.

53   Richard Rohr, *Jesus' plan for a new world*, St. Anthony messenger press, Ohio, 1996 pg.125

54   Eugene Peterson quoted in 365 *Meditations for Teachers*, edited by Anne Drew, 1996.

55   Thomas A Kempis, *The Imitation of Christ*, Bernard Bangley's modern English Translation, pg.78

56   Dietrich Bonhoeffer, *The Cost of Discipleship*, Prentice Hall & IBD; Revised edition edition (1963).